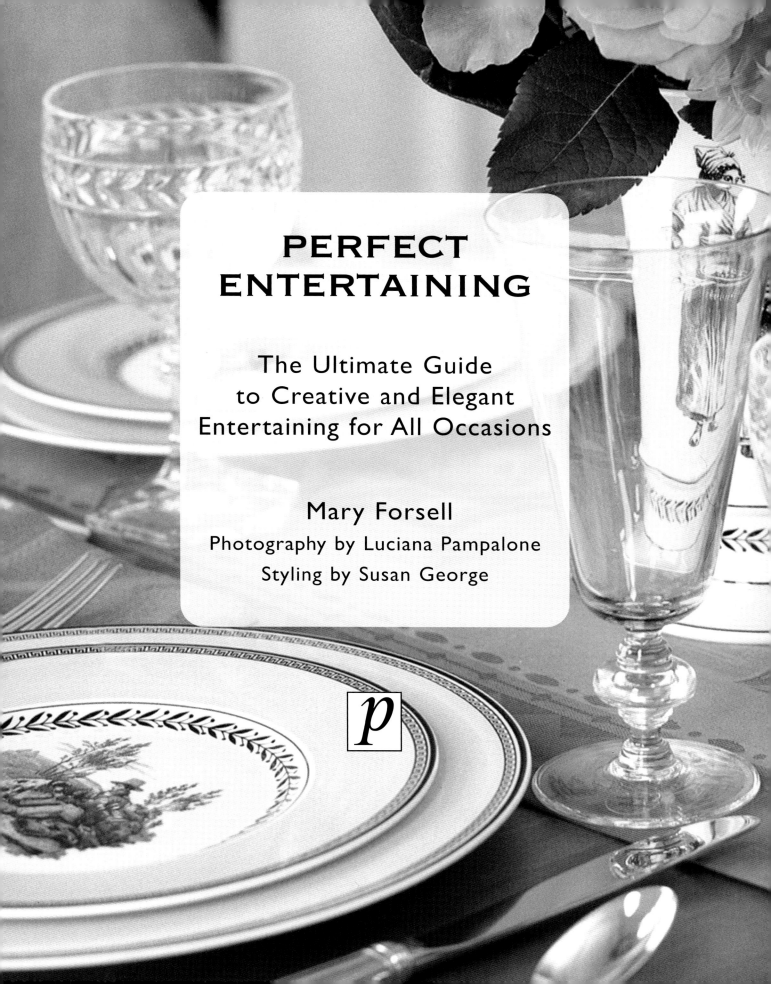

PERFECT ENTERTAINING

The Ultimate Guide
to Creative and Elegant
Entertaining for All Occasions

Mary Forsell

Photography by Luciana Pampalone

Styling by Susan George

p

This is a Parragon Publishing Book
Conceived and produced by Glitterati Incorporated/www.GlitteratiIncorporated.com

First published in 2006 by
Parragon Publishing
Queen Street House
4 Queen Street
Bath BA1 1HE, UK

Copyright © 2006 by Glitterati Incorporated
Text by Mary Forsell
Photographs by Luciana Pampalone
Styling by Susan George

Design by Anthia Papadopoulos

ISBN: #978-1-4054-7798-7

Dedication…
For Elizabeth Forsell, who is always entertaining

Acknowledgments
Tony Cenicola, for putting up with "the box of reference materials"
Marta Hallett, for conceiving the idea and making it all happen

PERFECT
ENTERTAINING

The Ultimate Guide to
Creative and Elegant Entertaining for All Occasions

Mary Forsell

Photography by Luciana Pampalone
Styling by Susan George

Contents

Chapter 1. Basics

For some of us, entertaining comes naturally. People can drop in and we'll always have something on hand. The secret to being a good host isn't charm, it's planning ahead.

There are two basic scenarios to entertaining: The first is that unexpected guests drop by and you have to pull together an informal gathering on the spot. The other scenario is the invitation, which enables you to plan ahead, including making a shopping list, placing food orders, reserving rental equipment, and planning the décor—including making sure you have enough seating.

3 DOZ EGG

Begin planning in advance. About a week in advance, shop for party items, frozen food, canned goods, and ingredients to make dishes. Prepare whatever dishes possible in advance. Check liquor supply and frequently used items and add whatever is necessary to the shopping list. This is also the time to buy candles and other décor and make sure table linens are cleaned and pressed. About three to four days in advance, you can move on to polishing silver (if it's a fancy party), cleaning seldom used dishes, making sure glassware is clean, and making food that can be frozen or will keep to the day of the party.

Two days before, clean the house, buy ice, do that last-minute ingredient check. On the day before the party, finish as much of the cooking as possible, rearrange furniture as needed, clear room for guests' coats, set up the bar, and have your coffee and tea service ready to roll. That means on the day of the party, you'll be ready to cook, put that white wine on ice and arrange your flowers. Just before the party, set out cheese or other nonperishable snacks, open red wine and mix first batch of cocktails or juices. Now relax and enjoy yourself (really)!

Informal vs. Formal Entertaining

Whether your guests are wearing tuxedos or jeans, there are certain "rules" that should be observed. First, be sure they're mixed and matched well. Try to establish what your guests have in common when you make your introductions. Just a tidbit of information can become a lively discussion after you've excused yourself. If someone seems left adrift, engage him in conversation and gently lead him to another guest with whom you think he shares an interest.

Periodically ask your guests if they need another drink or a glass of something else. Always provide nonalcoholic drinks such as seltzer, soda, juice, or sparking cider. And if it's a sitdown affair, once everyone is happily seated, don't delay picking up your fork and asking your guests to begin.

A Cook's Tools

If you're entertaining only small groups—for instance, six or eight guests—your family-sized utensils will serve their purpose. But if you're going for larger gatherings, say twelve or more, then you're going to need bigger supplies: party-sized casserole dishes, covered roasting pan, oversize soup tureens, holiday turkey platters.

Note that, except for cast-iron skillets, it is important that saucepans and pots are nonreactive stainless steel or ceramic to prevent chemical changes that occur when you're cooking with acidic ingredients like citrus juice, wine, vinegar, and tomatoes. Cooking with aluminum can alter flavors.

Everyone has a different cooking style, but it's undeniable that certain pieces of equipment make food preparation both faster and simpler. Why do things the old-fashioned way when there are short cuts. Among the equipment and handy gadgets that cooks swear by:

*Grater/Zestier

Go with the microplane rather than the boxy kind because it has many smaller holes. Truly, it's the only way to get delicate gratings from citrus and parmigiana cheese

*Knives

Invest in a few high quality steel knives and have a steel or stone sharpener. Knives that one must have are a chef's knife, utility knife, paring knife, and bread knife

*Euro Peeler

Much better than a traditional vegetable peeler, it lets you go more quickly and doesn't get clogged

*Immersion Blender

A long wand with a blade, this portable blender can be inserted right into a pot to puree and makes cleanup MUCH easier

*Spice Grinder

Buy an inexpensive coffee grinder and use it just for this purpose

14   Perfect Entertaining

A Cook's Ingredients

Keep these pantry and fridge staples on hand, and you'll always be able to whip up something special.

*Salt-cured Anchovies
These can be used to flavor salad dressings (such as Caesar), in sauces as a secret ingredient that enhances other flavors

*Vinegars
Balsamic (the best have the designation "aceto balsamico tradizionale di Modena" on the label), sherry, and tarragon

*Canned Tomatoes
Those that come from San Marzano, Italy are best. They're plum tomatoes available whole or crushed.

*Capers
Small addition that goes a long way

*Chipotle Peppers
Smoked jalapeno peppers come canned in a spicy sauce

*Eggs

*Extra Virgin Olive Oil

The best come form Italy, Spain, Greece, and France. Use it to finish dishes rather than as a cooking medium

*Five-Spice Powder
Chinese blend of cinnamon, cloves, fennel seed, star anise, and Szechuan peppercorns adds a lively spice

*Fresh Ginger

*Grapeseed Oil
A fabulous choice for sauteing because of its near invisible taste

*Israeli Couscous
It's actually a semolina paste that you can use in salads or add to soups

*Lemon Olive Oil
It's great to drizzle over seafood

*Olives
Whether you use them as an hors d'oeuvres or ingredients, they're indispensable. Green olives are harvested when grown but not ripe; black olives are ripened. Gaeta, Nicoise, Picholine, Moroccan, and Sicilian

*Pancetta
An Italian bacon, it's not smoked but cured in a combination of spices. You can use it in place of butter or oil and it freezes well

*Pasta
Imported dried Italian pastas are great in a pinch

*Pizza Dough

*Puff Pastry

*Rice
Especially arborio for creamy risotto

*Saffron
What would Spanish paella or French bouillabaisse be without it? Purchase threads rather than powdered

*Prepared Pasta Sauces

*Sea Salt

*Sesame Oil:
Essential to Asian dishes

*Soy Sauce
Also an Asian staple

*Onions and Garlic

*Stocks
Stocks can be time consuming to make, so buy unsalted chicken and vegetable stocks from the store and enrich it with aromatic vegetables

*Truffle oil
This can made by infusing olive oil with truffle and should be used sparingly

*Tuna packed in olive oil (good in a pinch)

*Variety of good quality cheeses such as Parmigiana Reggiano, and feta

*Walnut Oil
Adds a lively kick to soup

*Wine
For cooking and drinking

Basics

In a Pinch: Tips and Shortcuts

FOOD

Even busy people can cook from scratch by planning their kitchen time wisely and relying on today's convenience products.

Here are some of our favorite ways to make home cooking and entertaining quicker and easier than ever.

*Before starting any meal preparation, read all recipes thoroughly. You'll also save time by assembling ingredients and utensils before you begin.

*Rely on boneless, thin cuts of meat and poultry that cook quickly—usually in less than twenty minutes

*Convenience products give you a jump on cooking by doing some of the work for you. Items such as shredded cheese, minced fresh garlic, frozen chopped onions, precut vegetables, refrigerated doughs, and cubed meat for stir fries or stews often cost more, but the time saved may be worth the extra cost to you.

*Add favorite ingredients to quick-fix products. For instance, spread purchased cheesecake with seedless raspberry preserves and decorate with fresh fruit. Or make a simple main dish by stir-frying stirps of pork or beef, then adding a package of frozen Oriental vegetables and serving over rice.

*Make a mix unique with a few tasty additions. Top brownie mix batter with almond brickle pieces and chocolate pieces before baking. Ad orange or lemon peel or nuts to sweet muffins. Add chili peppers and shredded cheese to corn muffins.

*Go with flavor-building ingredients like infused oils and compound butters. For instance drizzling orange oil into a carrot-saffron soup. To be good, a dish doesn't have to have a ton of ingredients. Instead, simplicity can enhance the taste of food.

DECORATIONS

Equally important as the food you create for dining is the mood you set. Just a few minutes spent lighting candles or putting a favorite memento at the center of your dining table will make guests feel more than welcome and enhance the experience.

Here are a few staples to pull out in a second to create an inviting environment:

*Candles by the dozen

  Votives, tapers, pillars; dripless kinds for sconces and chandeliers

*Mirrors

  They create dramatic centerpieces with objects placed on top

*Throws, camp blankets

  To dress up the living room or set a picnic mood outdoors

*Mosquito netting for quick canopies

*Extra sets of inexpensive flatware, plates, and wineglasses

*Wooden, wicker, and silver trays for serving cocktails and hors d'oeuvres

*Cachepots, urns, and vases for instant floral displays—scour secondhand stores

*Paper lanterns from the Oriental supply store

  They're inexpensive but dramatic for creating a mood

*Strings of white lights

  Weave them through your potted plants, decorate the deck

Chapter 2. Breakfast

You might not think of breakfast as an opportunity to entertain, but it really is one of the most fun and charming times of day. Breakfast is a great way to celebrate birthdays, anniversaries, Mother's and Father's Day, or even the arrival of your latest houseguest. A key aspect of this overlooked meal is that, unlike lunch or dinner, breakfast is not dictated by conventions. Let loose with whatever creative frenzy strikes. Feeling slightly formal? Use porcelain soup bowls from your dinner service to serve cereal, with OJ in fancy stemware. For a funkier feel, break out your cow creamer collection as "bud vases" at each place setting. Take advantage of morning light and use colored glass plates in warm ruby tones to add a little drama to the breakfast table. Simple country touches could come from an enamelware pitcher and wirework egg basket—classics that are still being produced today. And, if the weather cooperates, set up the juicer, toaster, even the waffle iron in a prep kitchen on your patio or terrace.

Settings

At breakfast, the light is softer, the pace slower, the setting more intimate. Friends can gather around the table with the luxury of knowing they have the whole day ahead to pursue their passions, whether that be flea-marketing or touring fall foliage.

Celebrate that rare break in our busy lives and pile on the special touches: toast in a proper rack, soft-boiled eggs coddled in an old-fashioned egg cups, a spray of cymbidium orchids in a mint julep cup. Take a minute to finesse. Shape biscuit dough into shapes of a flower, offer fresh fruit with orange-yogurt sauce, sprinkle chocolate chips and banana slices into pancake batter.

You could create a tropical atmosphere with hot pink table linens paired with sunny yellow plates and an edible centerpiece of mangoes, pineapple, kiwi, and starfruit. For a citrus blitz, sprinkle pomegranate seeds and mint leaves on ruby grapefruit and present with silver grapefruit spoons. Alternatively, melt crystallized ginger on grapefruit halves under the broiler.

Make each place setting special. Here's a quick idea: fill a teacup two-thirds full with florist's foam, cut flower stems at an angle and insert. Use small flowers—miniature roses and clover, for instance—but use them abundantly to cover up the foam.

To signal that this is no ordinary breakfast, add importance with interesting seating. A picnic bench, church pew, or an armchair pulled up to the head of the table can completely change the look.

Omelette Know-How

Turn your breakfast into performance art with omelettes. The beauty is that they are so flexible—expand or contract depending on how large a crowd you're serving. When you're cooking omelets, you have to change the way you usually think about eggs. Instead of cooking them over low heat, go high and cook quickly.

The goal is to make it firm on the outside and creamy inside. The best part about making omelettes for a crowd is that they're made to order and everyone feels special.

Basic Omelet:

2 eggs

1 Tb water

1/8 teaspoon salt

freshly ground pepper to taste

1 to 2 tsp butter

1. In a small bowl lightly beat eggs, water, salt and pepper.

2. Melt butter in an 8- or 10-inch non-stick skillet with sloping sides over medium heat.

TIPS:

*Cover each omelet with foil to keep it warm while preparing additional omelets.

*Have plates—and guests—ready. Omelets need to be eaten fresh.

*Some cooks swear by allowing the butter to burn slightly before adding the eggs to the pan.

3. Turn heat to high and add egg mixture. When omelet starts to bubble and set around the edges (after a few seconds), run a spatula around the edge of the skillet, lifting eggs so uncooked portion flows underneath. When eggs are set but still shiny (after a minute or two), add filling, fold omelet in half, and transfer to a warm plate. Serves one.

FILLINGS:

Use any combination you love!

*Grilled or roasted eggplant peppers, and onions

*Cheese
 feta, swiss, cheddar, pungent, mild, or smoked, according to taste

*Mushrooms cooked in butter and sherry

*Fruit

*Salsa

*Minced herb combos, like fresh basil and chives with chevre

*Spinach sauteed in olive oil with diced tomato

*Crabmeat

*Lobster

*Cream cheese

A BETTER BUTTER:

*Blend an apricot butter to spread on toast and croissants: Reconstitute dried apricots in boiling water, then pulse in a food processor until finely chopped. Add softened unsalted butter and process until you have a sweet, smooth blend. Spoon into a decorative mold and chill.

*Try these other breakfast butters:

mint and dill

beebalm and lovage

lemon verbena and dash of grated orange peel

Fresh Starts: Buffets & Juice Bars

More often than not, breakfast guests don't appear on your doorstep—they straggle down the stairs, following the scent of coffee.

Fresh squeezed juice sparkles in a crystal carafe, French toast awaits in a footed compote, and a vintage cream pail holds cutlery. A dish of fruit, a vase of flowers, that's all you need to make a buffet sing.

A buffet glistening in morning sunlight will be a most welcome sight. All you need to do is set up a sideboard with tableware the night before and get the coffee pot brewing first thing the next morning. The meal could be as basic as croissants and muffins in a silver cake basket, a tray of fresh fruit arranged in fans, and pretty pewter mustard pots of marmalade and jam.

Stack hobnail milk glass pedestals on top of one another offering alternating tiers of fresh strawberries and muffins. To your guests, it will seem like a little b&b-style luxury, but it takes just minutes to do.

Take advantage of all the whimsical breakfast-related paraphernalia that's out there in antiques shops and at flea markets. Go formal with silver grape holders, orange cups, and banana stands. Or seek out transferware in tried-and-true informal color combination like red and white, blue and white, and brown and white. The beauty of using transferware such as this is that it all goes together and dresses up even the simplest breakfast of eggs and toast.

Even the most homespun pancake breakfast will take on a special quality when you serve it with Tiffany-pierced silver pancake servers—a popular item in the 19th century that is still available at antiques shops. So, too, there is a wide range of twentieth-century breakfast ware: streamlined deco services complete with teapot, toast rack, milk jug, and hot water pot; chrome jam cruets from the 1920s; and the endless array of cheery juice glasses from the 1950s.

Don't just go with the usual citrus suspects. Set up a fresh tomato juice bar. Or try these combinations:

*apple, guava, and pineapple

*banana, mango, and passion fruit

*mixed berries with coconut milk

*passion fruit with orange juice

Room Service

Want to pamper your guests? Then make life a little easier with breakfast in their rooms. There are so many fun but simple ways to make them feel at home.

Amusing as they are charming, eggs personalized with your guests' names using a gilt felt-tip marker show you went through a little extra effort. How else to greet guests? Write their names on garden plant tags plunked in a tiny moss- filled terracotta pots. Victorian brass place-card holders in the shape of hands can also hold name cards. "Monogram" natural objects, such as broad, flat stones. If guests will be on their own, leave them a map—perhaps one you've drawn yourself—pointing out places of local interest. Include a disposable camera so they can record their day. All on a tray. Add the local newspaper and a sunny nook to savor a quiet cup, and your guests will settle into vacation mode.

Set a tray with silver and a small wrapped gift for Mother's Day or a birthday. Sprinkle in other special touches like a dish of candied ginger or herbed butter for toast. Pick a bouquet of lilies of the valley, pansies, grape hyacinths, or any flower that takes to a teacup, then serve it to your beloved on a tray lined with a crocheted-edge placemat or teatowel.

BASIC BREAKFAST BAR:

Think hotel. On a counter or a table with a toaster nearby, set up the following:

* Plates, mugs, glasses, silverware and napkins

* At least two kinds of juice

* Decaf and regular coffees (clearly labeled)

* Assorted teas, including decaf and herbal

* Breads (such as raisin and multigrain), English muffins, butter, and jam

* Nonfat plain and vanilla yogurts

* Granola

* Cold celeral

* Bananas and seasonal fruit

Chapter 3. Weekend

Ah, the weekend. That's what it's all about, right? Dappled sunlight. The feel of summer grass between your toes at the country house. The smell of the surf and the call of gulls at a seaside bungalow. Or the crunch of snow under your feet at a Vermont cabin. Not that you need to have a separate place. The weekend is a state of mind, when long mornings and laughter-filled evenings reign.

Sounds dreamy, but none of this is yours to enjoy if you're the busy host who is running around trying to make everyone happy, not to mention cleaning up.

The secret of weekend entertaining is organize, organize, organize. You'll need big shopping lists and make-ahead plans. The more you can accomplish in advance—and the simpler the steps—the better. And the more you can get your guests to pitch in, the saner you'll be. Your mission: Enjoy and don't even think about Monday!

Warriors

The Art of Self Serve

Here's the game plan: Rather than running around at the last minute looking for supplies, make a shopping list to purchase either before leaving for your weekend retreat or just to have on hand.

Before guests arrive, get the dirty work out of the way. Wash and dry all greens and keep them chilled in sealable plastic bags. Measure out dry ingredients for scones, muffins, and coffeecakes in advance and put in sealable plastic bags. Grate and crumble cheese and keep them chilled in sealable plastic bags.

Gather a good cross-section of specialty breads like individual brioches, pumpernickel, and pitas. Supplement with a variety of prepared fillings so that you can set up a sandwich bar brimming with tempting combinations. "Help yourself" is your new favorite phrase.

When guests offer to pitch in, graciously accept their offers. Give some forethought to guests' abilities in the kitchen and assign tasks accordingly. Some might whip up salad dressings while others could chop root vegetables.

Sandwich Station

Offer a smorgasbord of possibilities for your guests. These fillings and combos should make life more interesting and fun.

*Smoked chicken with mango chutney on seven-grain bread

*Smoked salmon and cream cheese on pumpernickel

*Pan bagnat spread with Italian dressing, topped with onion, artichoke hearts, tomato, pepper, olives, and cheese.

*Shrimp, cucumber, and radishes with dill butter on pumpernickel

*Roasted red and yellow peppers with prosciutto, mozzarella, and balsamic vinegar on Italian country bread

*Tapenade, sliced tomatoes, and watercress on a croissant

*Grilled portobello mushrooms, eggplant, pepper, fennel, or squash on herbed bread

*Finger sandwiches on crustless white or wheat bread filled with cream cheese, grated cucumber, and minced dill

The Coffee Bar

Entertaining with a coffee theme is a world unto itself. You could set up a rolling pastry cart "bar" that allows guests to put together their own combinations. Equip it with an ice bucket and tumblers for icing coffee, wine glasses, and cinnamon sticks for Irish coffee, and an array of liqueurs such as anisette, cognac, and cointreau for adding to demitasse cups of espresso.

Chocolate syrup, coconut milk, fudge ice cream, whipped cream—all are accompaniments. Add a quirky sugar bowl and sugar tongs. Fill a jar with mother-of-pearl-handled demitasse spoons.

Convention states that the size of the cup dictates the strength of the brew. Smooth, light-bodied coffees are traditionally sipped from larger cups. Strong-tasting, thicker brews such as espresso are taken from smaller cups.

When you serve coffee in demitasse cups, remember that it is a double-strength brew. Espresso, by contrast, is made by a filtration method in which steam mingles with water, which is then pushed through the coffee for a smooth cup. Cappuccino is just espresso with steamed frothy milk. Add a mound of shaved semisweet chocolate and fresh whipped cream and you have chocolaccino. Cafe au lait or cafe con leche is served in bowls or handle less mugs, prepared by pouring equal amount of coffee and milk.

HOT DRINKS

First, reconsider your coffee paraphernalia. Drip coffee makers are convenient, to be sure, but they lack panache and are notorious for scalding coffee if the brew isn't transferred immediately to a thermal carafe. For entertaining, consider these possibilities.

Plunger

Often the choice of connoisseurs, plunger pots, also known as French presses, are noted for the rich coffee they produce, due to the slight application of pressure over the grounds, which are trapped under a screen. Metal screens are sturdier than nylon mesh. The trick is to bring water to a full boil first, wait five minutes, then pour it over the grounds.

Vacuum Brewer

Like a mad scientist's chemistry set, the vacuum brewer has double glass globes that ride piggyback. Water occupies the bottom globe, coffee grounds sit on top. Steam pressure forces water up through a cylinder from the lower to upper globe. As the air in the lower globe cools, a vacuum forms, sucking the coffee sludge through the filter and back into the bottom globe, offering a very dramatic, fun presentation for guests.

Multi-beverage Machines

Consider the new generation of combination machines, which whip up a menu of hot drinks made from premeasured pods or by reading bar codes on disks. They're great for pleasing a crowd. Multi-beverage machines serve up hot chocolate for the kids, hazelnut coffee for parents, tea for grandma.

Pump Espresso/Cappuccino Machines

To achieve the strong, heavy-bodied brew known as espresso and all its related drinks (cappuccino, latte, etc.), don't bother with stovetop makers or electric steam-powered machines. You'll need a pump machine. They can be tricky to operate, though the kinds that accept pods/capsules are more straightforward. They'll enable you to save a small fortune by preparing complicated drinks at home and are ideal for entertaining. There are espresso machines that grind primo beans to your specifications then whoosh out the perfect creme with the push of a button.

A PERFECT CUP OF COFFEE

Experts agree, the three Ts of coffee brewing are time, temperature, and turbulence:

*Temperature: Between 197.6-204.6

*F is ideal for brewing , 176-185

*F for holding, and 170-175

*F for serving. Drip machines certified by the Specialty Coffee Association of America (SCAA) meet these brewing and holding standards.

*Time: Drip machines with short brew cycles need a fine grind, while those with longer brew cycles require coarser grinds. Most machines do well with a medium grind.

Fine grinds: 1-4 minutes

Medium, drip grinds: 4-6 minute

Coarse grinds: 6-8 minutes

*Turbulence: The mixing action created by that water must be sufficient to saturate all the grinds. Look for drip machines that advertise a multi-hole sprayer head to ensure the grounds are in full contact with the water. Turn the machine over in the store—you can see for yourself.

Tea Every Which Way

You don't have to be a "tea person" to throw a tea-themed get-together. It's an easy way to entertain, and you can serve a choice of teas with a few items you've prepared yourself, sneakily supplemented by items from the bakery. Bridal showers, card parties, afternoon get-togethers are all occasions for tea.

Cups, Saucers, and Beyond

Think of teatime as an opportunity to put quirky and unusual servingware to use. Take out your collection of footed cake stands. Break out the mismatched china. Teatime is the perfect excuse to bring out specialized accouterments, such as a shell-shaped silver caddy spoon and tongs. Blue and white trans-ferware is always at home on the four o'clock table.

You could even serve tea in stoneware mugs, which spring from the tradition of high tea, that is, the English working-man's light supper of lunchtime leftovers. On an early spring day, why not revive the tradition with a dinner party featuring tea?

Afternoon tea, also known as "low tea," calls for your daintiest serving ware to serve crustless sandwiches and cakes. That's where the classic teacups and saucers come in, not to mention tongs to serve sandwiches, and a silver pot for pouring.

Choosing the Right Tea

With tea salons springing up every-where, it has become fashionable to look at the divine leaf in the same way we do food and wine—that is, match-ing the tea to the food.

The "cupping" of tea is how tea is eval-uated. And there is a great deal of ter-minology associated with tea grading. "Toasty" refers to aroma; "winy" to the mellowness; "brisk" to the "live" quality of the tea.

Use any terminology you wish, but do offer a few classic examples of the three basic kinds: green (minimally oxi-dized), oolong (semioxidized), and black (fully oxidized).

Let guests sample teas from individual pots, savoring the subtleties. Take this opportunity to show off a collection of interesting pots, from Chinese celadon to cottageware to a 1930's James Sadler & Sons English teapot shaped like a roadster. Tea is so much more than a drink!

As a rule of thumb for pairing tea with food, consider its origin. For instance, green tea from Japan teams naturally with seafood and sushi, as well as gin-ger-based dishes. A strong, smoky Lapsang Souchong, a type of black tea, works with hearty country cheeses. Earl Grey, a blend of black teas with a faintly citrus flavor, works well with desserts.

Iced Tea Accessories

For iced tea, use decorative glassware, such as candy-striped Murano glass, clear-stemmed or colored glass Italian swizzle sticks, perhaps topped by stripes or little balls. Also appropriate: silver iced tea sippers, which are silver straws with little spoons at the end. They're still available at flea markets and antiques shops. Of course, this is also a chance to use your glass pitcher collection, accessorized with sprigs of mint and bobbing slices of oranges and lemons.

Dessert Presentations

To host a large number of guests with ease, consider the dessert party. It's a perfect opportunity to show off a collection of cake stands—which have been popular since the 18th century—stacked in pyramids in order of decreasing size and arranged with sugared fruits, nuts, and patisserie. Try alternating more rare square types with round.

You could also set out wire-work egg baskets, trays, tiered stands, fruit and pie domes, cooling racks in a seemingly endless array of shapes and purposes. Today, the intricacy of the wire patterns makes the perfect decorative backdrop for presentations of sweets.

A fruit basket decorated with brass beads could become a holder for scones and cupcakes. Round or geometrically shaped tiered racks, which were once the popular method for allowing just-baked pies to cool, could hold fresh fruit or tarts, or simply present plates filled with tempting teatime creations. Even something so seemingly mundane as a hanging dish drainer, with a central niche for cutlery, could be transformed into a basket for fancy cookies surrounding a flower arrangement. A rectangular oyster basket with a wooden handle could become a biscotti server, and egg baskets are ideal for presenting macaroons.

Sweet Spreads

Dessert buffets are an easy—and delightful—way to entertain a crowd. Try these approaches:

*Seek out pressed glass cake stands from the 19th and 20th centuries. Not only did they come in green, yellow, and blue, but they also weren't necessarily round: square and cloverleaf designs proliferated. Stack a variety of colors and shapes on the table, filled with pastries, nuts, candied fruits, and petit fours.

*Nestle a checkerboard of truffles and silk flowers in a heart-shaped candy box.

*To delight children, fill lidded apothecary jars with a variety of confections: white-chocolate-covered cherries, bubblegum balls, peppermint sticks, and licorice whips.

*Construct "strawberry trees" by spearing whole fruits with toothpicks driven through to a Styrofoam topiary base.

*Create a sweet smorgasbord brimming with puddings, sugared fruits, tarts, and cakes. Serve them up in silver cake baskets and ceramic cake plates. Decorate the tabletop with a profusion of fruit, vines, flowers, and even spun sugar creations.

*Bundle flatware together with the napkin and tied with a floral fabric tie.

*Vary your presentation. Cake and cheese domes could mingle with garden cloches in a multilevel pastry "city." Stack pressed glass cake stands two stories high, topped by a vase of roses enclosed in a bell jar.

Cake Talk

Anyone who has ever planned a wedding knows: If you're going to serve a buttercream-frosted cake, be sure it's not going to sit out for long, especially in warm weather. Buttercream is notorious for melting. Fondant, on the other hand, holds it shape and can even be shipped long distance. Be forewarned if you're planning a dessert buffet in August!

Another consideration: Refrigerated or frozen cakes need to be stored airtight to prevent drying out or absorbing other food odors. The professional method is to wrap them first in plastic wrap, then in aluminum foil. That way you'll always have something fresh on hand.

A few presentation tips:

*When cutting a round cake, start at the center and work toward the edge. To ensure all slices are even, first cut the cake in half, then in quarters, followed by slices.

*Slice fruitcakes and pound cakes when they are cold for more precision

*Embellish plain supermarket cakes with your own icing and toppings. Before you frost, swab sugar syrup spiked with liqueur directly on cake for an added layer of flavor

*Hot, wet knives slice cheesecakes best. Wipe with towel after each slice.

*Pesticide-free edible flowers like roses, violets, calendula, and borage make for quick, impressive decorations.

Tray Chic: Moveable Feasts

Have big plans, but think small. That is, serve hold-it-in-your-hand-size foods that make it easy for guests to flow from room to room, such as mini plum cakes. "Which one is my drink?" is such a common question at parties. Supply guests with their own trays to customize with their own beverages and drinks, and you'll solve this problem instantly. Trays are a dime a dozen at thrift and secondhand shops, and you can always spruce them up with paint or decoupage. In fact, there is no shortage of metal cocktail trays from the 40s through the 60s, some with recipes for drinks or repeat motifs like clocks and roosters printed directly on them. Mini promotional trays from the past—given out by tourist stops like motels and gas stations—feature lithographed scenes. Their diminutive size is perfect for transporting appetizers from kitchen to table.

Chapter 4. Come fo

One of the simplest ways to entertain is the cocktail party. With a well-stocked bar and some cleverly devised hors d'oeuvres, you can pull off a party to remember without the need for a full sit-down meal or hosting an all-day event.

It could be as casual as, "Come for drinks and nibbles after work," or as formal as waiters passing hors d'oeuvres from trays. Somewhere in between is the spontaneous party. If that's your style, you'll want to have on hand a number of staples like hard salami and blue cheese, bread sticks, olives, sour cream for mixing with fresh herbs, and traditional cafe aperitifs that live permanently on a rolling cart.

cocktails

flirty

under the table

Come for C

please join us!

for
MARTINIS & MOJITOS
time
8 O'CLOCK TO ?
when
AUGUST 9
where
354 BROOME STREET
hosted by
LUCIANA & BILLY

Appetizer Wisdom

You want your guests to be wowed and delighted by the food. But, at the same time, you don't have an unlimited budget. There are some sneaky tricks of the trade you can employ to give your party panache without the price tag. Let's say you want to serve shrimp—an expensive food. Instead of placing out a heaping mound on a "help yourself" buffet, divvy them up on individual bamboo skewers. Add sophistication with exotic eats like eggplant "caviar" and Vietnamese summer rolls wrapped in rice paper—inexpensive yet impressive.

Streamline your presentation. By only offering finger foods like parmesan chips, Jamaican jerk chicken on skewers, or baby beef burgers and tiny sandwiches on interesting breads, you will cut down on plates and flatware. Guests will feel more relaxed and free to mingle since they won't have to deal with utensils.

If you are planning on having waitstaff, save yourself a bundle by using a rolling cart. It requires just one person to push it, yet holds dozens of small plates that would take an army to pass out.

Serve With Imagination

For appetizers that elicit "oohs" and "aahs," try these ideas:

*Tuck flower sprigs into florist's vials and nestle around the plate, disguised by lettuce leaves.

*Transform carrot slices into flowers: peel, remove stem and root ends, then use a mushroom fluter to cut a deep furrow down the entire length of the carrot. Rotate 1/8 inch and cut another furrow; repeat around entire carrot; slice into pieces or "flowers."

*Turn a tabletop into a frozen fantasy with an ice ring: place 1/2 inch distilled water in a ring mold and freeze until a thin coating of ice forms on the surface. Crack the surface with a spoon and arrange mint leaves, lemon, orange or cucumber slices, and fern fronds in the water. Return mold to freezer until frozen solid. Then add another inch of distilled water and freeze again.

Make-ahead Munchies:

Tomato bruschetta

Picnic-style deviled eggs

Creamy blue cheese endive boats

Caponata

Tiny crab cakes

Grilled toasts with herbed goat cheese

Recipe

Date-Almond Tapas

As guests bite into this impressive appetizer, they'll be delighted by the unexpected taste of almond, hidden away beneath each bacon-wrapped date.

16 pitted dates

16 almonds

8 slices bacon, cut in half crosswise

Preheat oven to 500 degrees. Put one almond inside each date, wrap the dates in bacon, and secure with a toothpick. Bake for 15-20 minutes, until bacon is crisp.

Cheese If You Please

A cheese tray is perhaps the easiest way to please a crowd. But it has to look as luscious as it tastes. Select cheeses with different flavors, shapes, textures, and colors. For instance, a rich Camembert and creamy Mascarpone would contrast with wedges of tangy gorgonzola.

Specialty cheeses, like peppered brie and muenster-cheddar, are another option. When pairing cheese with wine, remember, the more robust the cheese, the heartier the wine. For instance, sauvignon blanc or champagne with a young goat cheese or aged cheddar with cabernet.

Olives Anyone?

Olives are standard cocktail party fare. In Spain, they're the quintessential tapas bar food because they pair as well with cocktails as with wine. For full flavor, do serve them at room temperature. Choose a variety of colors and flavors—purple, brown, green, plump, petite. Picholine, Nicoise, and Calamata become heavenly aromatic after they are marinated overnight in olive oil, crushed garic, orange peel, and hand-torn sprigs of fresh herbs. Garnish with a few spirals of lemon zest. For contrast, serve them with dry-cured California olives or tiny, jewel-like Moroccan black olives. For fun, mix on a platter with various colorful raw vegetables and pickles—and not just the cucumber kind. There are also pickled onions, walnuts, and melon rinds that make a nice addition to an olive spread.

Classic Tapenade

This special tapenade is even better than the classic—its secret ingredient is pine nuts.

1 cup imported black olives, pitted

3 cloves garlic, crushes

1 T capers, or to taste

2 tsp pine nuts

4 T olive oil

1 T lemon juice

Freshly ground black pepper to taste

1 small loaf peasant-style bread cut into ½-inch-thick slices

Olive slices for garnish

Chopped parsley for garnish

Place all ingredients except the bread and garnishes in a blender or food processor and puree. Heat a broiler and toast the slices of bread on one side. Spread the untoasted sides with tapenade and broil for 3 to 5 minutes. Alternatively, spread tapenade cold on toasted bread. Garnish with slice olives and parsley. Makes about 1 cup; serves 2-4 as an appetizer.

Art Of The Raw Bar

The raw bar packs a visual punch that far outweighs the effort of putting one together. Assemble a variety of containers ranging from galvanized or copper washtubs to baking trays and broad, open baskets (lined with plastic). Fill with an ocean of crushed ice. Then decorate with seaweed, edible, pesticide-free flowers, horseradish leaves and other tasty edibles from the herb garden. Now you're ready to bring out the fruits of the sea—a smorgasbord of shucked clams and oysters on the half shell, cooked, cold scallops, mussels, and shrimp. Have lots of condiment choices, ranging from spicy cocktail sauce to minced chiles, fresh pepper, lemon and limes for squeezing, horseradish, and a delicate mignonette sauce. Offer buttered black cocktail bread squares if desired.

Come for Cocktails

The Well-Stocked Bar

It's time to take stock. For a bar that can function smoothly at a cocktail party you'll want to include basic spirits like gin, rum, vodka, tequila, and whiskey—the building blocks of mixed drinks. To treat connoisseurs, you might also have a single-malt Scotch on hand for quaffing. Go with larger, 1-liter bottles for entertaining.

Next up are spirits and wines, such as dry and sweet vermouth, brandy or cognac, and red and white wines that are not too pricey or fussy. In other words, good party drinking wines that everyone can enjoy. Your local liquor store can certainly suggest a few to buy by the case, possibly at a discount. Beer, of course, is also an option—even if you don't plan on making it the focus of your party.

Then it's on to the liqueurs, depending on what you'll be serving: cointreau or triple sec for margaritas, Kahlua for black Russians.

Don't overlook the nonalcoholic ingredients such as juices (cranberry, grapefruit, and orange juices in large bottles); a variety of soft drinks; canned tomato juice or Bloody Mary mix, and of course, club soda, tonic, and bottled water, both still and sparkling.

Condiments and garnishes should round out your liquor cabinet. Lime juice, Angostura bitters, Worcestershire sauce, hot sauce (such as Tabasco), coarse salt, superfine sugar for coating glass rims, cocktail olives, onions, and maraschino cherries.

HOME BAR ESSENTIALS

If you're serious about cocktails, then
you'll need these items on hand. Store
bar supplies in a cabinet together with
the liquor. Also consider a small refrigerator, which comes in handy for wines and
vodka, the latter is a particular treat
when stored in the freezer.

*Cocktail shaker with strainer
 Metal shaker covers a strainer that fits
 onto a metal cone

*Electric blender
 For whirling up frozen drinks and crush-
 ing ice

*Jiggers
 This helps you measure. With two cones
 at either end for holding different standard amounts of liquids.

*Bottle opener

*Corkscrew

*Ice buckets, scoops, and tongs

*Pitcher

*Decanter

*Stirrers

GLASS ACTS

The home bartender needs an array of glasses, but not necessarily everything noted on these pages. Since most cocktail recipes do note the type of glassware that should go with it, you'll pretty much always know from reading a recipe what you'll need. Decide what sort of entertaining you'll most likely be doing and outfit your cabinets accordingly.

Above all, the most versatile glass is the cocktail glass. It can easily move from chilled, neat drinks to martinis and frappes. Also known as a martini glass, it's basically just a conical shape and should always be chilled.

Bigger and rounder than the martini glass, the margarita glass is perfect for serving that favorite Mexican drink and has a wide diameter so that you can easily rim it with salt.

You'll also want to have champagne flutes—those familiar tall, tapered glasses designed to keep bubbles bubbly longer because there is a minimum amount of surface area exposed to air. They're also nice for champagne cocktails.

Champagne can also be served in wide-brimmed glasses—the kind that Marilyn Monroe would have used.

Whichever you choose, the champagne glass should be as thin and delicate, since thicker glassware will raise the temperature.

Highball glasses—a.k.a. tumblers—are flat bottomed, plain-looking glasses that hold between eight and twelve ounces. Ideal for mixed drinks, they are generally used for highballs, Tom Collins, bloody Marys, beer, and soda. Lowball glasses (a.k.a. old-fashioneds or on-the-rocks glasses) are also tumblers, but shorter. They hold between five and ten ounces and are also used for mixed drinks like gin-and-tonics, old-fashioneds, black-and-white Russians.

More specialized glassware that you might like to have on hand: Snifters for liqueurs are meant to be cupped in your hand so that your palm actually warms the liquid. They have a classic blown glass shape. Irish coffee glasses have handles for holding hot cocktails like hot buttered rums and hot toddies. Aside from being served in a highball glass, beer is traditionally passed in straight pilsner glasses as well as in English pint glasses.

Though wine can be a complex, complicated subject, wine glasses are the contrary. Keep them plain and simple. Go with the tulip shape, with a wide bowl that tapers toward the top so that it traps aromas. Glasses should have stems for ease of swirling and so that your hand doesn't come in contact with the glass and change the wine's temperature. In other words, always pick up a wine glass by the stem, not the bowl.

Believe it or not, there are no rules set in stone about glasses for red vs. white wine (with the exception of the champagne glass, of course). In general, white wine glasses tend to be a fluted cone shape, while red wine glasses are squatter and more bulbous. Some Europeans drink red wine from tiny little tumblers. Let your aesthetic be your guide.

World of Wine

Traditionally, there is a wine for every food. White wine has long been a favorite partner for seafood, salads, and lighter fare, while red wine goes well with red meats, pasta dishes, duck, and game. Over the last several years, these rules have been consistently challenged. Today's thinking overrules these considerations in favor of personal preferences, since the heaviest white wine—for instance, a barrel-aged chardonnay—is "weightier" than the lightest red wine, such as a Beaujolais or Valpolicella. Still, certain wines have undeniable affinities for specific foods. And, generally speaking, it's best to go from light to dark when serving a meal.

White wine, usually produced from white grapes (but not always) should be served chilled. Common white wine grapes vary greatly. Chardonnay is the sans pareil white wine grape. The best examples are opulent, lush, rich, and buttery and pair well with simply prepared chicken, veal, or pork dishes. Less full-bodied than chardonnay, sauvignon blanc lends itself to many foods; thus, making a good all-purpose wine. Chenin Blanc, often blended with other grapes, varies from dry or extra sweet. It is a summertime casual quaffing wine. Riesling, a German wine, tends to be delicate and sweet (though there are drier versions) and works well as a dessert wine as well as with Asian dishes. On a similar note, GewÅrztraminer, often left for late harvest to bring out its richness, is often seen as a dessert wine but also works well with spicy dishes. Muscadet is the quintessential French seafood wine. Semillon is often blended with sauvigon blanc, and Viognier from France is a rich dry wine.

Red wine, by contrast is made from red, purple, or blue grapes. The color comes from the contact with the red grape skins during fermentation. Its flavor tends to be richer and deeper than white wine (indeed, there are wine connoisseurs who don't even recognize white wine as a category!). Served at a warmer temperature than white to let its complex flavors unfold more fully, it can be chilled briefly—say 10 to 15 minutes.

As with white wine, there are many different grapes that go into the mix. One of the best known, cabernet sauvignon, has an intense black currant-and-cedar wood flavor. It works superbly with red meats, especially lamb, and any dish with complex, assertive flavors. Gamay is a lighthearted, berry-tasting wine from France's Beaujolais region that is best enjoyed while young. Grenache is a gorgeous velvety grape that typifies Rhone wines. It works well with strongly flavored foods like grilled sausages or spicy sauces. Merlot, which blends well with cabernet, has a similar flavor profile but softer.

Pinot noir has black cherry, raspberry, and a spicy profile and, when mature, can take on the aroma of game and truffles—it's the quintessential turkey wine. Sangiovese is an Italian bombshell, robust and full-bodied. Syrah/Shiraz (depending on where they're produced) partner pleasingly with game and spicy stews.

Tempranillo is a full-bodied Spanish native that works well with simple grilled meats. It is one of the key grapes of Rioja. With its taste of ripe berries, Zinfandel is the unofficial state grape of California. Use it as you would a cabernet. Rose is a pink-colored wine made when the skin of red grapes is left in contact with the juice for a short period of time. Usually made from the Grenache grape, these pink-tinged wines should be served chilled and complement most anything, especially seafood.

Sparkling wines are created when a yeast and sugar solution is added to dry table wine. The fermentation creates tiny bubbles of carbon dioxide. Only wines produced in the Champagne region of France can be termed Champagne since they are produced using the time-consuming, multi-step method Champenoise. Sparkling wines go by the names Blance de Blanc, Spumante ("sparkling" in Italian), and Cremant.

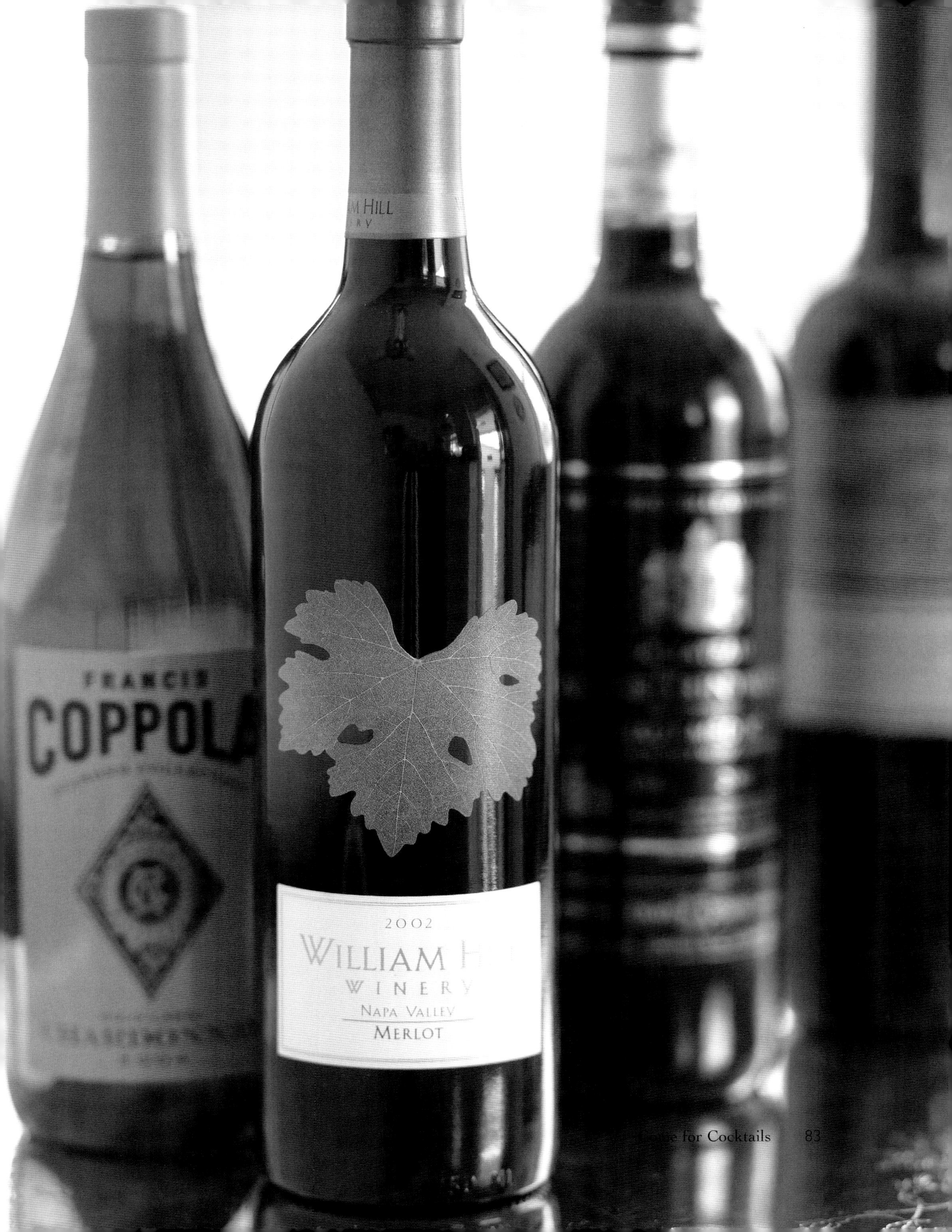
COPPOLA
2002
WILLIAM H
WINER
NAPA VALLEY
MERLOT

Inexpensive (But Good) Wines To Try

When you buy by the case, retailers will often shave ten or fifteen percent off prices. Plus, you can sometimes return unopened cases for a refund (check local liquor laws). Tip: Save up to seventy-five percent by choosing a sparkling wine over a true Champagne. And don't think that imports are necessarily more expensive. The following are all reasonably priced nondomestic choices:

Montes Reserve, Sauvignon Blanc, Chile (white)

Marques de Riscal, Rueda, Spain (white)

Palacio de La Vega, Tempranillo Reserva, Spain (red)

Jaume Serra, Cristalino Extra Dry Cava, Spain (sparkling)

Nine Stones McLaren Vale, Shiraz, Australia (red)

Kanu, Chenin Blanc, South Africa (white)

Domaine Houchart, Cìtes de Provence Rose, France (rose)

Sieur d'Arques, Cremant de Limoux Toques & Clochers, France, (sparkling)

Mionetto, IL Prosecco, Italy (sparkling)

Vallebelbo, Moscato d'Asti, Italy (sparkling)

Drink Dressups:

Powdered Sugar, Garnishes, Ribbons, and Charms

*Garnish drinks with lemon balm leaves and curly orange zest

*Add borage flowers, pineapple mint, and curly spearmint to a red punch

*Dip glass rims in lemon juice, ther twirl them in colored sugar

*Tie ribbons around the stems—different

colors help guests remember which is theirs

*Float cranberries in sparkling water

*Use fun straws

*Customize star fruit wedges in heart shapes using cookie cutters to customize

*Make small glasses out of ice and serve shots in them. Serve with a cotton napkin

*Add scoops of sorbet to ice a drink

*Hollow out plum tomatoes or blood oranges and serve drinks (bloody Marys and mimosas, perhaps) inside, sipped from mini-straws.

Recipes

MOCKTAILS & OTHER NONALCOHOLIC TRICKS

Just because it's a cocktail party, it doesn't mean people have to consume alcohol. Offer a selection of alluring alternatives. Let your inner mixologist come out and play. Most drink recipes can be made without liquor simply by leaving it out. Alternatively, you can dress up drinks in a convincing way with fruit-flavored Italian syrups for look-alike, taste-alike drinks.

TEA ON THE ROCKS

Brew iced tea and serve in old-fashioned glasses. Add a wedge of lemon and a mint or lemon balm sprig for garnish.

JUICE JULEP

The beautiful thing about this mocktail is that you can easily turn it into an alcoholic drink with a splash of rum.

1 quart chilled unsweetened apple juice

1 cup chilled unsweetened pineapple juice

1 cup chilled orange juice

¼ cup chilled lemon juice

Mint sprigs for garnish

Combine juices in a 2-quart pitcher. Mix well and serve in tall glasses filled with ice cubes. Garnish each glass with a sprig of mint. Makes about 1 ½ quarts.

CRANBERRY SPRITZER

It's cool and elegant—and it's good for you.

1 ounce cranberry juice

1 ounce orange soda

4 ounces club soda or seltzer

lemon slice

Fill an old-fashioned glass with ice. Add sparkling juice mixture and garnish with lemon.

FAUX PINA COLADA

1 ounce coconut syrup

3 ounces pineapple juice

1 cup ice

Pineapple wedge for garnish

Combine ingredients in a blender, pour into a highball glass, and garnish with pineapple wedge.

Chapter 5. Dinner Part

Do the words "dinner party" strike fear in your heart? Do they bring back memories of being trapped in your childhood room, as the clink of glasses, smells of roast, and chatter of adults drift upward? There is much mystique around the dinner party. A way of entertaining groups with a little more flair than, say, an afternoon cookout, the dinner invitation has a lot of baggage. There is more etiquette associated, more ways to "go wrong."

Not to worry. We've mapped out the proper way to pull it off, even if you don't know a water glass from a red wine goblet. Once you get the hang of it, you'll be throwing parties right and left.

Calm down. Invite your guests into the kitchen to have wine with you. Don't worry about being perfect. And keep your sense of humor. If you're uptight, everyone else will be too. Relax and enjoy yourself. Remember: the ideal number of dinner guests is eight to twelve—just enough to keep the conversation lively and flowing.

Know-How

Choosing A Theme

So much depends on dinner, as the expression goes. But when planning the menu, so much more depends on the season. If you live in a cold, wintry climate, devise ways to enjoy the season with hearty, flavorful foods shared with people you care about. Snuggling by the fire with food and friends is one of the best ways to celebrate the season. Hearty meals designed to fuel outdoor activities like skiing and skating rule. Aside from the holidays, there are a jillion excuses for winter parties: host a sledding or snowman-making party or throw out all the stops for Valentine's Day, the Super Bowl, Marci Gras, even Elvis's birthday (January 9!)

Come springtime, longer days and a feeling of restless anticipation bring out those "bites of spring," like baby vegetables, lamb, fresh asparagus, and lighter meals. Here is a time of renewal, with parties that emphasize new beginnings. A few excuses: Major League Baseball opening day, a yard sale, Cinco de Mayo, the Kentucky Derby, and, of course, Mother's Day.

Summertime is all about grilling and lounging outdoors. You'll find plenty of suggestions for decorating in the next chapter, but keep in mind that this is all about the bounty of the season: fresh fruits and vegetables, homemade berry ice creams, grilled freshly caught fish with summer vegetables, like corn and zucchini. Summertime themes include the tiki party, Memorial and Labor Day bashes with patriotic touches, pool party (BYOB—bring your own bathing suit).

Of course, autumn is all about bounty—a time of glorious color, crisp, clear air. It's the season to be thinking of stews and soups, of baked parsnips and herbed roasted turkey. Expand your offerings beyond the expected Halloween party to host an Oktoberfest, mark the end of daylight savings time (break out the candles and the hour glasses) and raise a glass to Sadie Hawkins Day (November 13th), when women turn the tables on men.

Planning A Menu

A meal has to function on several levels. On the one hand, it should be nutritious. On the other, it should taste as good as it looks. To achieve this harmony, you'll need to do a little thinking. It's all about balance.

Start with the main course. If you're going with something spicy, like chili or a peppery Mexican dish, side dishes should be considerably milder. However, if the dish is subtly spiced and delicate, the side dishes also shouldn't eclipse it. Think of how to balance your entree with one starch like potatoes, pasta, or rice paired with greens, for instance.

You also need to balance the temperature of the foods—hot and cold. Think also in terms of varied textures, such as crisp with soft. Make sure your meal has a healthy dose of color and interesting shapes. Dessert should also complement the meal. For instance, you wouldn't want to serve brownie sundaes after a four-cheese lasagna. On the other hand, a light meal can end in a rich dessert.

To keep stress levels to a minimum, prepare what you can in advance, go with tried-and-true recipes (no last-minute experimenting!). Unless you'll be having outside help from a caterer or an on-site chef, don't plan a complicated menu. If need be, supplement it with prepared dishes from the local specialty market.

CROWD-PLEASING CLASSICS

Perhaps the most crowd-pleasing, economic, and, above all, versatile dishes around, pastas and risottos are a great bet for a dinner party.

Risotto Revolution

Risotto is the ultimate comfort food of Italy. Chefs never seem to tire of trying new combos. The key to its success is the constant stirring action, which draws out the creaminess and texture of the rice. This is a classic dish for adding new twists. Risottos rely on your choice of stock or cooking liquid absorbed by the rice. Chicken, veal, mushroom, and vegetable stocks are all possibilities. Some chefs have been known to use pure vegetable juice in lieu of stock to intensify the flavor. When making risotto, keep the broth hot so the risotto is simmering at a lively pace.

The six steps to perfect risotto:

1. Have stock simmering on the stove

2. Melt butter

3. Caramelize onions

4. Add rice

5. Add wine and stir until it's been absorbed. Add stock in small increments, stirring until it's absorbed

6. Toss in final ingredients, such as cheese and herbs and any precooked chicken, seafood, and the like

Here are some fun add-ins:

*Pesto with walnuts

*Beet greens with lemon juice

*Sundried tomato or black olive puree

*Shrimp and peas

*Zucchini with fresh basil

Pasta Aplenty

Pasta needs no introduction. But there is so much more to try than you've probably ever imagined. Beet pasta, black pepper pasta, saffron pasta...there are more flavors to choose from than ever before.

A few pointers:

1. Have a gallon of water for every pound of pasta

2. Don't go by the cooking times printed on the packages. Fresh pasta could be done in as little as thirty seconds or so, and dried pasta after four minutes. Keep checking until it's tender yet firm with a tiny white center

3. It's best served on warmed plates

Some wonderful combinations to serve a crowd:

*Olive oil, walnuts, and Parmigiana cheese

*Cream, prosciutto, and peas

*Roasted peppers, tomato, and fresh basil

*Shrimp, butter, and lemon juice

Mix and Match Sauces

*Cheese tortellini mixed with pesto sauce and baby spinach, which will wilt upon contact with hot, cooked tortellini. Serve immediately or at room temperature.

*Farfalle with lemon-asparagus sauce: bowtie-shaped pasta simply dressed with tender asparagus and fresh lemon juice and topped with crispy garlicky bread crumbs.

*Radiatore provencáale: fresh vegetables, such as tomatoes, eggplant, and bell pepper, impart the flavors of sunny Southern France combine with radiatore-shaped pasta. Cook the vegetables in olive oil with garlic and onion in a separate pan and mix together.

*Tofu stuffed shell salad: cook pasta shells and prepare a filling: mix tofu in a bowl with celery, mayonnaise, dill, salt, and pepper. Or mix avocadoes, toasted walnuts, walnut oil, and fresh lemon juice. Chill both salads until ready to serve.

*Macaroni with ricotta salata and basil: Ricotta salata is a sheep's milk cheese. Crumble it into an elbow macaroni salad with tomatoes, basil, salt and pepper, toss and drizzle with olive oil ad vinegar. Serve at room temperature or chilled.

Wok 'n' Roll

The wok is China's answer to one-pot cookery. The workhorse pans of China for at least two millennia, the wok is ideal for stir-frying, it heats evenly and its upward-sloping sides minimize spills. Plus they cook a meal quickly, in as little as five minutes, enabling guests to enjoy the show.

A few pointers:

* Use high heat and the shortest cooking time. This sears food and lets it cook quickly, without drying out. Never crowd the pan because this reduces the temperature of the pan.

* Fourteen-inchers are ideal. Smaller than that, and food doesn't have room to move around. Larger and it doesn't heat up enough.

* When cooking, heat the wok to the point of smoking BEFORE you add the oil. Then, once you add the ingredients, let them sizzle for at least twenty seconds to a minute before you start moving them around.

* You'll need to prep everything before starting because the cooking process is quick. Cut all your ingredients into uniform sizes, so they'll cook in the same amount of time. However, cook thicker, tougher vegetables like broccoli and carrots longer than delicate, leafy vegetables.

*Add all sauces in final stages.

*Bags of cut vegetables from the supermarket save time but be sure they're absolutely bone dry. Otherwise, they will steam instead of stir-fry.

Fondue Revival

It's back. People are rediscovering fondue, that dinner party staple of the 1950s courtesy of Switzerland. You'll love it. The dish begins in a saucepan on your stove but then is transferred to a fondue pot. It's basically a pantheon of melted cheese flavored with white wine and, possibly, kirsch. Then bread, meat, or other chunky ingredients get dipped. There is also a dessert variation, which involves fruit dipped in chocolate.

*For silky smooth fondue, soak cheese gratings in white wine for an hour or two prior to cooking

*For too-thick fondue, turn up the heat, add a little white wine, and stir

* For too-thin fondue, dissolve cornstarch into white wine and add, stirring under high heat

*For dunking, go beyond bread cubes: blanched vegetables, mushrooms, and pear and apple slices, salami cubes and pepperoni wedges, baby artichoke hearts, red bell pepper slices, and zucchini wedges

*Fondue connoisseurs dip their bread cubes in kirsch before cheese.

*Do mix cheeses; for instance, swiss, cheddar, and gruyere.

*Sweet, dessert fondue combinations might pair ladyfingers, whole strawberries, and peach wedges dipped into chocolate

Dressing The Table

How to Lay Dinnerware and Flatware

Though the size of the place setting has expanded and contracted over the last two centuries, the number of utensils always corresponds to the number of courses and are arranged from the outside in. That is, place the plate in the center of each place setting. Forks are placed to the left of the plate (except for the very small fish fork, which goes to the right). The spoon and knife, with its blade side turned in toward the plate, go to the right of the plate. Place bread-and-butter plates to the left of the dinner plates just above the forks. If you're serving salad, places plates to the left of the forks.

Depending on your preferences, of course, you could add dessert spoons and forks and coffee spoons horizontally along the top of the plate or just bring them to the table for the dessert course. For French settings, the forks and the soup spoons are deliberately placed upside down to show off the decorations on their backs. As is customary, dessert utensils sit above the plate.

Glassware is arranged left to right in order of size: water, red wine, white wine, dessert wine/sherry. Place them

above the knife on the right of the plate. Place cups and saucers to the right behind the glasses. For that final touch, place an attractively folded dinner napkin on or above the dinner plate. It's also correct to fold it in the water glass. If the dinner plates are going to be served warm at the last minute, simply place the napkin directly on the table.

That having been said, there is an alternative method in which silverware is placed on the table in order of size. Settings look more symmetrical when silverware is placed in order of largest to smallest. This is considered a little more contemporary.

For buffets, which are generally reserved for groups of eight of more, stack dinner plates next to the main course, with side dishes nearby. Place serving utensils, such as salad tongs,

alongside the dish. Depending on how the traffic flows, place napkins and flatware at the end of the line or even set actual tables for guests.

Accordingly, you could place glassware on the buffet or on the dining tables. You can definitely improvise with buffets in terms of what goes where. There could be a section for desserts, for instance, or they could go on a separate table.

To stay on schedule, set out everything the night before.

From Pottery to Porcelain

So much mystique surrounds the all-important dinnerware pattern. How to pick the right one? Plain or patterned? Bold colored or neutral? Modern and sleek, country, or traditional?

Before you push the panic button, remember: It's in the mix. You don't have to have a set of all-matching china to set a table. You might mix rustic stoneware with contemporary, deep-hued Asian-look plates in triangles and squares. Pull out your grandmother's fine china and crystal, but mix it up with bamboo and rattan accessories if you so please.

Even with this casual, eclectic attitude, however, it's nice to know the "rules"

before you can break them. In other words, know what you're shopping for and then decide how—and if—to mix it up.

When an object is made from fired clay, it is considered a ceramic. Within this category, there is a polyglot of terminology having to do with the type of clay that is used to make the ceramic and the temperature at which it is fired. Among the many subcategories of ceramics are pottery (also known as earthenware) and porcelain, the true china (though now the term is used to describe a broad cross-section of ceramics).

To identify porcelain like a pro, do this test: Hold it up to a bright light. If you can see your fingers on the other side, then you are likely holding a piece of porcelain. For centuries, porcelain production was a Chinese secret. Then European producers cracked the code in the 18th century. Their first attempts resulted in soft-paste porcelain, which was translucent but not as durable as hard-paste porcelain, which is fired at a higher temperature. Somewhere between hard- and soft-paste porcelain, bone china is yet another variation, said to have been invented by Josiah Spode in the 18th century.

If you were to hold a piece of earthenware up to the light, you'd find that it isn't translucent. It is also more easily broken. Slipware, stoneware, delftware, ironstone, transferware—all are forms of earthenware. Transferware, in particular, is a lot of fun to mix and match in a rainbow of colors—blue, mulberry, black, brown, green, and even polychrome.

Collectors can't get enough of the vividly glazed pottery known as majolica, first introduced in the 1850s by Herbert Minton. Cauliflower-shaped sugar bowls, lettuce-leaf plates, "wicker baskets" filled with fruit molded in relief; realistically decorated seashells resting on painted nests of seaweed...the range of whimsical designs is remarkable and are sure to add personality to your table.

In this century, designs such as chintzware became popular beginning in the 1930s. Printed with tiny flowers all around in the manner of the cloth for which it is named, chintzware adds a delicate look to the tabletop.

The Italian love of long, leisurely meals and spirited conversation gave birth to faience in the mid-16th century. Still going strong, this everyday earthenware decorated with opaque-colored glazes is ever appropriate, easing oh-so-gracefully from lunch to dinner, indoors to out. Blue faience pairs well with a summery cotton striped fabric, as it does with a damask linen cloth.

Silverware

When you think "silver," does a lavish tea service displaying gleaming and polished on a sideboard come to mind? Certainly, it's a pretty picture (if you can afford it), but there's a world of silver out there to collect piece by piece without breaking the budget. Bud vases, toast racks, creamers, marmalade spoons, cake knives, asparagus and sugar tongs, powder jars, pomanders, and salt cellars are among the jumble of silverware you'll typically find at markets, priced so reasonably it's irresistible.

Among the most sought after pieces are British silver and silver-plated items such as napkin rings, teapots, vinaigrettes, and salt cellars. During the last quarter of the nineteenth century, in particular, these objects became imbued with exotic or romantic motifs, such as cupids and other mythological figures. Today, they make charming conversation pieces on the table, particularly on Valentine's Day and other romantic occasions.

Many people shy away from silver collecting, believing that it is too temperamental to clean. But it really isn't all that difficult to care for. Silver that is

marked "sterling " is a standardized alloy of 92.5 percent silver and 7.5 percent copper (or 925 per 1,000 parts pure silver). Silverplate, by contrast, is a base metal that is electroplated with silver.

When true silver turns black, you are seeing silver sulfide—a reaction to humidity as well as sulfurous foods, like eggs, salad dressing, and vinegar. The common sense solution: Clean silver quickly to avoid stains. If possible, keep it in a glass case to minimize humidity. Never store in contact with plastic, which can leave black marks. In fact, acid-free nonabrasive storage materials are essential. To wash, use a mild dishwashing detergent, rinse through, and dry and polish with cotton flannel. To remove tarnish, use only a mild polish, such as a gentle silver foam—forget those "immersion" type cleaners that remove the patina of age. You especially want to show them off in your silver's nooks and crannies.

Love of Linens: How and When to Use Tablecloths, Napkins, Placemats, and Runners

There is no rule specifying that you have to use a tablecloth, placemat, or runner. However, napkins are de rigueur. Dinner napkins are the largest of napkins, measuring about twenty-four inches square at the largest. Napkins for other meals—breakfast and lunch—tend to be smaller by a couple of inches. Cocktail napkins are the tiniest, measuring about four by six inches.

By all means, steer clear of all white. For instance, when you choose a loose-weave linen, playfully ornamented with stripes in an unexpected color like pink, you bring elegance and a relaxed air to the table all at once. Rather than going with an all-white scheme, pair white damask napkins with a tablecloth embroidered with colored thread for a more casual look.

Then there are the many textiles that await creative reuse.

Vintage dish towels with classic red banding are a case in point, particularly the French types, which come in a variety of shapes. The square ones make nice placemats; the longer, narrow types are perfect as table runners. If you find a supply of vintage kitchen linens in similar colors, use them as napkins, perhaps with a classic striped Basque country tablecloth. Drape them over small tables offering hors d'oeuvres, line a tray for a drinks table with them, or tuck them into a basket when you serve muffins and breads. For truly casual meals, bandannas also make good napkins.

Blankets are also perfect table partners. For a cozy winter dinner, toss them over tabletops and strew fringed throws over chair backs. Ticking is a classic rough-and-tumble material also that does well on the table today. Originally a covering for matteresses, linen or cotton ticking is durable and meant to take some wear, which is why it's such a perfect choice for a tablecloth at a summer home, paired with gingham napkins and cheery crockery or china.

Consider, too, the possibilties of fabric from afar. Moroccan, Central American, and Balinese textiles, for instance, all seem to go together. When you combine textiles from various countries, think about the common denominator: color and pattern. Surprisingly, you'll find a strong similairy between African and Scandinavian design in that they both use natural materials, emphasize hand-weaving, and feature strong hues and simple designs. So you could use cloths from Mali and Marimekko alike to cover tables at an outdoor event, each featuring bold color blocks.

Nowadays, a wealth of linens from the past can be had at flea markets, auctions, and estate sales. Among the most captivating and timeless are monogrammed designs, which come from a time when every girl learned stitchery at her mother's knee. When you discover a cache of monogrammed textiles in your antiquing travels, by all means, scoop them up, regardless of the letter they depict or even the purpose they serve. All can be brought to the table with charming results.

For instance, an early 20th century batiste sheet embroidered in high relief with petals and leaves and an initial at center could serve as a tablecloth or even as an outdoor canopy. Monogrammed tea towels from the 1930s could "slipcover" cafe chairs: sim-

ply fold them over the tops of the chairs and anchor them with ribbon tied through the hemstitched openings. Initialed cotton handkerchiefs are charming stand-ins for for table napkins. Sturdy ecru linen dishtwels with letters in crosss stitch emboridery make homey placemats.

Candlelight

As professional caterers, restauranteurs, and event planners well know, candles are the least expensive way to transform a room. They are always more dramatic in a large group, and you can multiply their effect by setting them on a mirror or placing them on a mantel over the fireplace with a mirrored background. In fact, you can decorate with a whole glittering constellation of candlesticks of different sizes and materials: crystal, glass, metal, pottery. To unite them all, use the same candle in each, perhaps a classic ivory-toned beeswax taper.

Also rummage in your cupboards for alternatives. Celery holders, hurricane glass chimneys, and footed ice cream dishes make for an intriguing display. Eggcups and orphaned teacups are perfect for votives, while flowerpots turned upside down and fitted with tapers in the drainage hole are quick yet imaginative tabletop solutions.

You might even dress up candle holders with tiny necklaces of crafts store beads strung on wire. When you group a variety of candles in related colors together, you're guaranteed a pretty look. Go ahead and mix crystal, metal, and ceramic holders. To create a mesmerizing mood for an evening gathering, pair all-white candles with pale flowers, which will seem to glow in the dark.

More possibilities: Float votives in a pottery punchbowl and set on the kitchen counter, a pedestal table, or a wooden crate. Floating candles also look wonderful bobbing in a collection of clear glass cylinders. In wintertime, bring the display outdoors with glowing lanterns. Candles decorated with foliage, hot glued in place, wink and gleam on a silver tray, which can be transported anywhere for instant aura. Displayed on a tiered stand, honeycomb votives, roses, and white turnips draw guests to a wine and cheese buffet.

Not Just Flowers: Ideas For Centerpieces And Place Settings

First, know that there is absolutely no rule on the books that says a tabletop must have a crystal fruitbowl flanked by two candlesticks.

 A collection of wooden spools of varying sizes makes for an architectural tablescape. Arrange a collection of colored glassware down the center of a table in a serpentine fashion. Display a collection of found natural objects on top—moss, acorns, pods, and stones. A shallow pewter bowlful of carpet balls with a red and white theme makes a cheery accent.

Bring freesia and tuberoses in vases to share the table with pots of rosemary and passionflower. Place little pots of herbs on a tiered etagere. A tableside baker's rack filled with canning jars holding tuberoses will charm as much as a centerpiece. Or simply float blossoms in footed bowls. Think jasmine, lemon flowers, and gardenias.

Nonfloral Centerpieces

Feather boas are fun and funky. They're especially useful if you have a color scheme that's hard to create in flowers—for instance, black and white. White flowers combine with black feathers.

Fruits and nuts create a Dutch still-life look. Small, delicate fruits like kumquats and little acorns and pinecones, even strawberries look pretty with flowers.

Use mirrors to extend the arrangement, whether underneath or behind to double the effect.

March eucalyptus leaves down the table's center, interspersed with seasonal fruits like pomegranates, pears, and persimmons

Whatever you choose, keep the centerpiece low so that guests can see each other, which stimulates conversation.

Use flowers, to be sure, but mix them with fruits like persimmons and pears.

Palette Pleasers

When designing floral centerpieces, go with something other than the usual suspects. Consider these combos:

*Magenta, hot orange, & cameo pink. Two strong colors offset by a paler one really sing. Try magenta hydrangeas, orange mums, and pale pink roses.

*Chartreuse 'n' chocolate It's a sophisticated, understated look. Try cocoa brown and green calla lilies with hypericum berries and chocolate basil.

*Monochromatic drama. For instance, roses, amaryllis, and poppies look smashing, especially with a crystal chandelier overhead.

*Urban/downtown: calla lilies, orchids, pitcher plant, chocolate cosmos, poppies, ranunculus, carnations,

*Country/woodsy: black eyed susans, daisies, sunflowers, zinnias, yarrow, Queen Anne's lace, corn flowers, Mexican sunflowers, ferns, grape hyacinths, pansies, lilacs, hydrangeas

*Elegant: French tulips, orchids, roses, peonies, stephanotis, lilies of the valley, lisianthus, sweet peas, French anemones, gardenias, Dutch hydrangeas

*Beach/seaside: black eyed susans, zinnias, daisies, ornamental grasses, rambling roses, cosmos, hydrangeas, cattails

Four-Season Punch Bowl:

Rim a punchbowl with a floral wreath. Make it on a wire wreath base set on a glass tray or pizza pan. Wedge Oasis foam into the wreath base, secure with floral wire, then place sprigs of plants in place. The Oasis foam keeps the flowers fresh. Vary the look with the seasons.

Summer:

boxwood, artemesia, lamb's ears, fever-few, yarrow, beebalm, lilies

Fall:

Goldenrod, dried globe amaranth, sweet annie, staghorn sumac

Winter:

juniper and ivy

Spring:

grape hyacinth, mint, elderflower, daffodils

Pleasures Of Place Cards

Who knew? Entertaining etiquette dictates that when you have six or more guests, you should use place cards. Don't be intimidated! They can be simple, handmade affairs or something more creative:

*Plain manila tags double as place cards and gift tags when dressed up with dried flowers and attached to a beribboned token on a plate.

*Calligraphy place cards might also sport small drawings, stenciled motifs, or paper-punched designs.

*Tucked under a sheer napkin and embellished with gold ink, a place card takes on a mysterious air, like an unopened letter.

*Trim place cards with lilies of the valley and rest them on herbal nosegays held in silver tussie-mussies,

*Spell guests' names in cloves on an orange.

*Write names on shells.

*Your best friend just published a book? Decorate with a literary theme: a centerpiece of stacked classics or a low vase of tasseled bookmarks. Make bookmarks as place settings or collect check-in cards from old books.

*Insert craft wire into corks and make a double curlicue on top. Tuck name cards into curlicues.

*Use collection, such as small chairs to balance cards.

Serving Vegetarians And Vegans

There IS a distinction between vegetarians and vegans. Vegans consume no meat or animal products—including eggs, dairy, and honey. They also do not use animal products in any way, so no leather placemats. By contrast, there are many kinds of vegetarians—some eat eggs but no dairy—but what they all have in common is that they don't eat meat.

There's a good chance that you're going to have at least one vegetarian or vegan in the crowd, so be prepared. Have dairy substitutes on hand, such as soy cheese, soy yogurt, and "milks" made from rice, soy, or nuts. For instance, have soy or rice milk available at a breakfast bar. For soups, forgo chicken- and beef-based stocks for tasty prepared vegetable broths.

Thicken soups with a pureed mixture of cauliflower and white beans. Use nondairy, bean- or vegetable-based dips like hummus and babaganoush. Pastas don't need cheese to shine: dress up yours with roasted grilled vegetables. Opt for intriguing sauces like tofu "ricotta" or miso chile. We've all been conditioned to think of meat as the centerpiece of a meal, but vegetables can easily take on that role.

Think roasted beets with assorted squashes in a hazelnut vinaigrette. Or roasted brussels sprouts with caramelized walnuts. Serve a fiddlehead fern and morel salad with walnut oil and vinegar. Marinated tempeh cutlets served with Chinese vegetables could easily please a crowd. It's amazing how many possibilities there are that don't involve meat or dairy.

Chapter 6. The Great

Outdoors

As soon as the weather warms, no one can resist living outdoors. Here, entertaining takes on a whole new dimension, as the sights and sounds of nature enhance your gathering. That's why, in many ways, it's easier to take your party outside. When friends drop in, you need little more than a table with ticking yardage and a few rustic collectibles. The trick is to use tableware and furnishings already in your house or basement in creative, even whimsical, new ways.

Let's say you're throwing a summer dinner party that begins with cocktails in the barn. For the seated meal outside, ask each of your guests to grab a chair, crate, or haybale and carry it to the field, where a farm table awaits. The drama comes from the surprising contrasts: perhaps there is already a splashily slip-covered armchair set amid the grass. The table beckons with white china and violet goblets sparkling on a humble linen mesh cloth. Add birdsong and a glorious sunset, and you've made magic.

Setting A Garden Party Mood

In planning your party, work with the landscape. If a corner of your yard is planted with ornamental grasses and variegated foliage, then break out the rattan trays and baskets and wicker-wrapped bottles to enhance the 'natural' theme.

For a flower-filled border or rose garden, get out all your petal-themed china and knickknacks. Use a retro rose tablecloth and prop a trellis or two behind the buffet for the full effect. Similarly, a gazebo or Asian-style teahouse might inspire Blue Willow china as serving ware.

To accent a rockery, rustic stone wall, or a sculpture garden, fill galvanized buckets and pails with river rocks and stones (you can buy them by the bag load at the local home center) and use them as accents here and there.

For a magical atmosphere, hang "charms" from tree branches— Christmas decorations, like hearts and stars, vintage keys, tiny silver cups, chandelier prisms. Paper lanterns and strings of twinkling white lights are always a propos.

Organizing Buffet Stations

Chances are, your yard wasn't designed as a party space. But with a little planning, you'll be able to create a fluid environment where guests meet and mingle. Be sure to designate bar, buffet,

and sit-down dining areas to keep people circulating. If possible, lay out your buffet table—without food, of course—the night before, covered with a plastic tarp, so that you'll be as ready as you can be.

What buffet table, you say? It's probably already in your own backyard. For instance, you could turn the potting shed into a serving station for a garden party. Wipe down your work table, add a roll of unhemmed fabric as a tablecloth or a humble linen mesh cloth, and you're in business. A washtub could become an ice bucket for champagne.

Alternatively, create a freestanding serving station. Use sturdy poles with hooks to raise a makeshift tent overhead (it could be something so simple as an Indian-print cotton bedspread)

Your outdoor buffet could also consist of a hodgepodge of household tables. Unify the look and cover odd-sized tables using a simple roll of fabric directly off the bolt, fringing the edges and puddling the fabric on the ground.

Patio Decor

Add a little esprit to your patio or deck. Funky pillows, floor cushions, and ottomans all lend themselves to the outdoor 'lounge' look—and many are available in stain- and weather-resistant fabrics.

Don't hesitate to bring out "real" furniture: armchairs, a rug, an end table or two. Use folding screens as a backdrop for the bar. Paint wicker furniture fire-engine red, and forest green and haul out all paint-worn furniture and yard sale finds. It creates a surprisingly intimate atmosphere.

For an instant table runner, layer yardage in varying widths. A coarsely woven undyed linen or hemp over burnt orange raffia, with ends fringed by hand, has a rustic, Provençal aura; pair it with folkloric crockery.

Everyone knows that blue sends a cooling message to the brain, so when the mercury rises, think aqua, teal, and spruce. Paint a picnic table blueberry and you'll shave a few degrees instantly. Ambitious? On its own, a chipped old bench is hardly worth noticing. But flank it with topiaries, add candle sconces on the wall behind, and pile on the pillows and you've created a focal point.

Beach Bound

One of the special perks of an ocean- or lake-side party is the built-in entertainment. Beachcombing, wave riding, canoeing, and fishing all become part of the activities. When you take your party to a beach—whether by the ocean or by a lake—you'll have a few more considerations. You'll probably want to bring a grill, though the lion's share of the food would be best prepared beforehand.

Decide in advance whether you'll eat on the ground, perhaps on a carpet of boldly printed Indian textiles or some other interesting cloth. Or bring in lightweight folding tables and beach chairs to keep the sand out of the food. Dressed in checked or striped fabric anchored with vases of wild-flowers, your beach setting will have undeniable appeal.

Pots of sea grass marching down the center of a picnic table would be ideal at a clambake, perhaps with a hurricane lamp at the center surrounded by seashells. Fill a spongeware bowl with sea urchins. Or for a lazy-day lakeside grill, decorate with old creels and fishing nets.

For the finishing touches, define the party area with tiki torches or candle lanterns created from mason jars filled with sand. Stick pinwheels in the ground to catch the breezes.

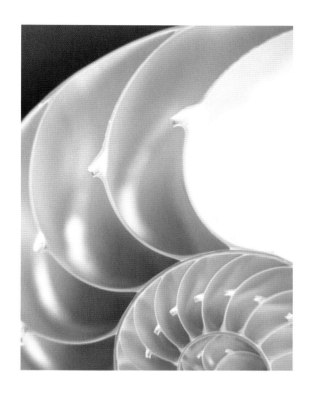

Pool Party Panache

Think cool. Galvanized metal accessories like pails and minnow buckets are great for chilling bottles. Cleaned-up metal garbage can lids turned upside down and filled with crushed ice make a fun presentation for seafood hors d'oeuvres.

Above all, be sure to use unbreakable cups if you'll be serving around the pool. A wonderful alternative to glass that fits with your cool-pool theme are retro aluminum cups from the '50s (available at collectibles shops).

Centerpieces Alfresco

Summer flower arrangements are the essence of simplicity. Wildflowers in pop bottles. Single leaves in jam jars. Or just strew sunflower or zinnia heads with stems snipped off.

Try sunflowers in a watering can, butterfly weed in an enamelware coffee pot, gerbera daisies and gaillardia in a painted bucket.

Why limit yourself to one vase when you can enjoy a half dozen? Vintage milk bottles in their original metal holder make a rustic counterpoint to elegant garden roses. Nestled in a garden hat, potted culinary herbs make a charming, fragrant centerpiece.

Live plants still in their terracotta pots are decorative, and you can plant them afterwards. Take a few sunflower plants still in their pots and swathe the bases in burlap—which looks great along a buffet.

Baskets filled with a single fruit—limes, oranges, pears, or apples, for instance—are both economical and edible. For a fancier effect, line baskets with banana leaves and palm fronds and use them to present food.

Tailgate Time

Not all outdoor gatherings take place at the height of summer. On a crisp fall weekend, a tailgate party is a novel way to entertain. Come autumn, everyone's appetite seems to grow, so be sure to plan a menu that satisfies. Perhaps a Southwestern turkey chili, vegetable wraps with a dipping sauce, some spicy Chinese noodles accented with chunks of chicken, a tin overflowing with luscious, freshly baked cookies, and steaming thermoses of soup and coffee.

For a stylish statement, tote your lunch in a fancy old-fashioned wicker picnic basket (though a cooler works just fine). Set up a lightweight, portable table spread with a cozy blanket in a sunny spot—with a view of a blazing patch of fall foliage nearby. Metal bread bins make great portable containers for crusty sandwiches and breadsticks. Little tinware lunchboxes are handy— and stylish—for transporting condiments. Wire cooling racks are perfect for presenting old-fashioned bar cookies and brownies.

Hammered aluminum trays serve well to pass food around, while antique wooden breadboards with carved details make attractive portable work surfaces when you don't have a picnic table.

ALTERNATIVE GRILLING

Charcoal is great, but there is a whole underworld of on-the-grill flavorings that is yours to try. You could strew grapevines, seaweed, and herb sprigs into the flame or place them directly on the grill. Or lightly crack your choice of nuts—almonds, pecans, walnuts—and toss them on the fire. A favorite in the American South, fruit tree wood chips are another great bet. All of the above need to be soaked in water for a half hour before going on the grill. If you prefer gas grills, look for the types with a compartment designated for aromatic wood and herbs.

To make a bouquet garnish for scenting smoke: Bundle together fresh parsley, thyme, bay, tarragon, and marjoram and tie with raffia. Hang upside down in a dry room with good air circulation for 2 weeks.

Flavored Oils for Flair

The secret to using flavored oils is to use less because they pack such a flavor punch. As a rule of thumb, use half the amount of oil you ordinarily would. For instance, a salad that serves four and takes 2 tablespoons of oil only needs 1 tablespoon of flavored oil.

To make a flavored oil:

On low heat, heat olive oil, peanut oil, or vegetable oil until the fragrance begins to waft out; this takes about 5 minutes. Then pour the oil into glass jars with stoppers. Fill with ingredients of your choice, and let steep for one hour. They can be stored for up to three days in the refrigerator. We like:

*Oregano, thyme, and olive oil
*Chervil, tarragon, shallots, and peanut oil

*Fresh ginger, cardamom seed, coriander leaf, and safflower oil

*Dill and sunflower oil

*Basil, chili, and olive oil

*Lemon verbena, lemon thyme, and walnut oil

Burger Revisited

Set up a burger bar with choices old and new: grilled or raw onions, sliced tomatoes, grated cheddar, bacon or ham, sliced avocado, lettuce, mustard, ketchup, chili sauce, relish, herb butter, and mushrooms and onions sauteed in butter. Offer toasted English muffins and a selection of French and rustic peasant-style breads.

*Spinach burgers: Add chopped spinach and mashed chickpeas to the ground beef for a moister burger

*Lamburgers: Add chopped parsley and nuts of your choice and grated onion to ground lamb; top with roquefort

*Mexican burgers: Combine ground beef with chili sauce and cayenne pepper

*French burgers: Combine ground beef with burgundy (about ¼ cup per every 1 ½ pounds) and pinch of dried thyme

Outdoor Party Activities

Keep the party rolling from afternoon well into evening. A few ideas and tips:

*Involve the kids in shucking corn

*Set up a croquet lawn, badminton net, and hopscotch board

*Provide butterfly nets: the perfect "catch-and-release" activity

*Fill a trunk with sunglasses, straw hats, shawls and jackets for when the temperature dips at night

*Light up a row of citronella candles and scatter stick-on bug-deterrent around tablecloths. Each guest could also receive a bug-away bracelet (available at outdoor stores and drug stores).

Chapter 7. Holidays

Entertaining takes on a grander dimension when it's centered on holidays. Rather than merely serving a meal, you'll be creating memories and carrying on nostalgic childhood traditions, perhaps with your own twist.

There are a number of simple strategies to make your life easier during this potentially stressful time. In planning the menu, go with simple-to-prepare recipes. Your old favorites will work perfectly, so long as they're presented with panache. Or plan on updating a standard recipe with a new twist, like a sprightly fruit sauce instead of traditional gravy. Prepare as much as you can a day or two in advance. That way, on the day of the party, you'll only need to reheat dishes or making simple side dishes.

Well before the day arrives, take inventory of tables and seating. If your dining table isn't long enough to serve as a buffet, use the kitchen island instead. Or plan on putting a door on sawhorses and cover with an attractive tablecloth. Ask friends and neighbors for folding chairs if you think you'll need extra seating, or rent them from a party-supply house.

The night before, set out platters and serving bowls to guide traffic flow. Place large plates near entree dishes and smaller plates near side dishes or appetizers. Set up a beverage station on its own table.

On the day of, don't go it alone. Let the whole family get involved. Teenage children could serve as waiters and candle lighters, while younger kids could greet guests and take their coats to a coatroom. They could also have fun dressing up the family pet to greet guests at the door.

Open-House Tree Trimming

It's a lot of fun to get everyone involved in trimming the tree. You'll find your kids even more engaged in the process if cousins or friends are on hand. Or maybe your decorating style needs a breath of fresh air and could benefit from the input of holiday guests. By all means, invite a crew of all ages and pull out all the stops to make them feel welcome.

Establish a welcoming note by lighting the way with luminaries made from ordinary brown lunch bags. Simply fill with one inch of sand and add a votive candle. They'll provide beacons of cheer on a dark winter's night while also lighting the way for arriving and departing guests.

Rather than limit decorations to the living room, sprinkle them through practically every room of your home. Ordinary household objects need only minor additions twist to shine. When you fill teacups, trophies, and compotes with vintage glass tree ornaments or collectible figural glass light bulbs in the shapes of Santas and snowmen, they instantly get into the holiday spirit. Even if you don't have vintage collectibles on hand, you can still create a memorable setting.

Classic tissue paper snowflakes could decorate windows, while paper partridges perch in a reproduction feather tree. Paper chain garlands created from gift wrap could decorate mantels, banisters, and powder room windows with plenty of charm.

Of course, if you expect revelers to trim the night away you have to feed them well. Several choices of soup would be most welcome on a buffet. Think pumpkin-leek, vegetable, beef-and-noodle, and other nourishing blends, served from big pots with ladles. Treat guests to a "soup bar" of garnishes, including freshly grated parmesan, minced scallions, croutons, salsa, cheese sticks, whole shrimp, toasted pumpkin seeds, pomegranate seeds, sour cream, and pine nuts. As well, offer a festive punchbowl garnished with lemon slices and set on an evergreen wreath. And what would the holidays be without plenty of hot chocolate in carafes? Position a tray nearby with peppermint and cinnamon sticks, which can be used as stirrers and will subtly flavor the beverage.

Before coffee is served, create a batch of sugared spoons, coated with melted white and dark chocolate, then dipped in colored crystals. Or serve a dessert with a decorative border on the plate. To do so, spoon melted chocolate into a pastry bag fitted with a #4 tip. Now pipe a holiday greeting on a dessert plate rim.

Dessert can look special without labor-intensive baking. Simply layer luscious ingredients in pretty parfait glasses. Go for ice cream or whipping cream, candied orange peel, store-bought pound cake, fruit preserves, chopped nuts, sprinkles. Even more decadent are layers of chocolate mousse and bakery

brownies, topped with chopped toffee bars and nuts. Keep it interesting by providing contrasts of crunchy and smooth, sweet and salty.

Recipe

Almond-Garlic Soup

For a surefire hit on a chilly winter's night, try this warming, soul-satisfying soup. This recipe serves 6.

1 pound sliced or slivered blanched almonds

3 hardboiled egg yolks

1 pint vegetable stock

1 pint light cream

2 cloves garlic, minced

Salt and freshly ground pepper to taste

Yerba buena, mint or apple slices for garnish

Pound the almond and egg yolks together (preferably with a mortar and pestle) to make a paste. Put the almond paste in a saucepan over low heat and very gradually add the vegetable stock, stirring constantly to keep the soup smooth. Add the cream, garlic, and salt and pepper and stir well. Continue stirring until the mixture is very hot, but not boiling, about 10 to 15 minutes. Pour into serving bowls and top with a garnish of your choice.

On Christmas Morning…

If you have overnight guests for the holidays, set them a special breakfast table. Pile a tiered stand high with kumquats, pomegranates, and other appealing fruits nestled among shiny ornaments. Make each place setting special with green napkins cinched with mandarin-colored ribbons. Equally festive are napkin rings made from strands of prestrung glass beads or flatware simply tied with a silver ribbon.

Just for the fun of it, offer a diner-style menu you've printed up on the computer. It could be decorated with stamped images and bound with holiday ribbons—or let the kids create their own.

Use cookie molds to make tree- or wreath-shaped pancakes ornamented with strawberry "bows."

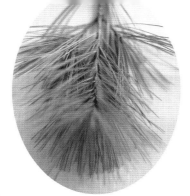

Wreaths, Garlands, and Display Ideas

Southerners and Californians have long known that you can get that Christmas feeling without the usual suspects of holly and ivy. Instead, French flower buckets overflowing with pineapples, baskets of citrus, and pots of paper whites and ornamental cabbages encircling the tree (or a sled and Adirondack chair) get you in a natural mood while a simple concoction of cinnamon sticks, clove and allspice simmers with water on the stove. A planter filled with hyacinth pots nestled neck-deep in moss with pyracantha berries spilling over the sides is a far cry from the expected poinsettias.

Instead of the usual citrus clove pomander, try one gleaming with beadwork or turned into a votive holder. Down-to-earth decorations include eucalyptus banister garlands entwined with safflower pods, ferns, and lemon leaves or humble glass containers wrapped in raw silk and festooned with fresh roses and snow berries from the yard. For a fresh-from-the-woods look, swag grapevines over doorways accented with sprigs of cockscomb and dried floral bundles. Trim the tree with cranberry stars or chicken wire everlasting bouquets and swath it in a burlap tree skirt in a petal shape.

There are so many fresh ways to go: Grass green and peony pink gift wrap...cards strung on jute roping, interspersed with jingle bells, pinecones, and pomegranates...votives tucked into hollowed-out apples or artichokes set on the windowsill...a make-it-yourself holly topiary dangling with gilded cardboard fruits or favorite seashells...corrugated paper gift wrap festooned with tiny pine cones...faux floral "collars" for lampshades...potato print stockings ...birch branches coaxed into a wreath and dusted with gold glitter.

Sparkly decorations also rule, like rock candy wrapped in thin cord or wire as tree decor. Plunder your costume jewelry collection for inspiration—trim a tiny tree with rings, necklaces, earring, bracelets and brooches that feature stones in the colors of peridot, citrine, amethyst, aquamarine, and topaz. Pin brooches on stockings. Fill a candy jar with Christmas tree pins, stars, and Santas.

In southern Europe, holiday homes are filled with lemon blossoms and peri-winkle. Recreate this effect with arrangements of fresh flowers such as birds of paradise or fragrant freesia. Pile bright orange kumquats in a tall clear glass vase and use the fruits to anchor the flowers. Make a quick, fragrant ornament that speaks of Mediterranean shores by intertwining a rosemary cutting with lavender in a small circle and tying with ribbon. Or use a wire frame to create a larger wreath using these materials.

Stroll around your yard looking for interesting greens to harvest. Juniper, white pine, boxwood, and holly are all candidates. Just by plunking them in galvanized buckets, you'll put the house in holiday mode. Fill out the effect with potted paper whites and amaryllis.

In winter, night comes early, so opt for decorations that do best by candle-light—for instance, a amaryllis center-piece could provide a bright spot of color by day. Come evening, it could be exchanged for a sparkling (and edible) display of sugared fruit.

Try this recipe: Gather pears, champagne grapes, lemons, and figs. Dip whole fruits in lightly beaten egg whites, sprinkle superfine sugar over them, and arrange on a cake stand. Add sprigs of fresh greenery. You can't eat this arrangement because of the egg whites, but it's still delectable to the eye.

For still more nighttime shimmer, string white fairy lights everywhere—around doors and windows, on banisters, and bookshelves. Spiff up anything that shines, especially brass and chrome. Add bows of silver Mylar or silver organdy to potted plants, entwined with gleaming jingle bells.

Party Flavor Fun

Who can resist a party favor? Especially when your hosts made them just for you. Sun-cooked strawberry preserves, apricots dipped in chocolate, green peppercorn and tarragon mustards, sun-dried tomato pesto, infused oils, and vinegars—all will be so much more appreciated than off-the-shelf store-bought presents. Display them all on a "favor" bar in a corner of the living room, perhaps with the recipient's name or monogram on an accompanying tag. For an unusual presentation, bake the same-shaped cookie in three different sizes, for instance star. Stack on top of one another from largest to smallest and tie with a ribbon. They make sweet mementoes from a wonderful day.

Truffles or any homemade candies are sweetest presented in fluted foil or paper cups (available at candy supply stores) and stored in a single layer in an airtight container. Decoupage the container with images cut from giftwrap or with photo copies of old letters or vintage recipe book illustrations.

Orange Chicken Breasts with Pomegranate

Pomegranates are in season just around the holidays, so the next time you're having a crowd over, consider this healthy, flavorful dish instead of the usual turkey or ham. This recipe serves 6 as a main course or 12 as a light buffet offering.

Marinade:

1 cup freshly squeezed orange juice (about 3 large oranges)

4 tablespoons Aurum (an Italian liqueur), orange liqueur, or cognac

Grated zest of 2 oranges

½ teaspoon freshly grated nutmeg

¼ teaspoon ground cardamom (optional)

Entree:

6 whole boneless, skinless chicken breasts, halved

Salt and freshly ground pepper to taste

Flour for dredging

1 egg, beaten

Fine, dry bread crumbs

Olive oil

Canola oil

2 tablespoons sweet (unsalted) butter

Grated zest of 1 orange

Seeds of 1 pomegranate

Chopped Italian (flat-leaf) parsley for garnish

Mix all the marinade ingredients together in a glass bowl and marinate the chicken for at least an hour. Drain and reserve the marinade. Pat the chicken dry with paper towels and season with salt and pepper to taste.

Dredge the breasts in flour and shake off any excess. Dip in the egg. Let the excess drip off, and coat each piece with bread crumbs. Pour equal amounts of each oil in to a sauté pan to a depth of ¼ inch and heat on medium heat. Sauté the chicken on both sides until brown and cooked through, about 5 minutes per side.

Remove the chicken to a serving dish and keep warm. After all the breasts are cooked, discard the oil and add the butter, reserved marinade, and orange zest to the pan. Bring to a boil over high heat and reduce until the mixture thickens, about three minutes. Add the pomegranate seeds and season with salt and pepper. Pour the sauce over the chicken, sprinkle with parsley, and serve.

Springtime

As the season's first blush of vegetables ripens outside, the urge to bring these fresh tastes indoors is irresistible.

Spring dinners emphasize the classics— lemony sorrel, sweet-tart rhubarb, tender baby peas—to awaken our palates, and our longing for warmer days ahead. Think local goat's milk cheeses with wine-washed crusts...pastry filled and topped with chantilly cream and strawberries…tender baby vegetables to add color and crunch.

Whether you're celebrating Easter or Passover with family, observe tradition, yes, but add contemporary twists. Grandmother's recipe for potatoes au gratin could get a flourish of aromatic fennel, carrots could be glazed with ginger, and peas might trade an ordinary butter sauce for one flecked with freshly snipped herbs. Or try a cold kiwi soup in the exact shade of spring grass. Prepare in advance in whole or part, which not only intensifies the flavors but frees you to savor the day.

To dress the table, go with a pastel garden palette: lilac dishes, a lavender silk tablecloth, and gentle green glassware. With the addition of real flowers to set them off and a potting bench as a sideboard, your dining room becomes a slice of garden life. When you add contrasting textures—a cherrywood charger, an Indonesian teak tray, spun bamboo baskets, flatware with mother of pearl or bark-style celluloid handles, rustic beeswax candles—you create an aura of tranquil rusticity. Theme your china to the season. A great example is cabbage ware, which was originally developed in Sèvres, France, in the 18th century. Named for its raised borders resembling the ruffly edges of a cabbage leaf, the gilt floral china will always be at home at spring garden parties.

Grilled Salmon with Chive Butter Sauce

Get an early start on grilling at your next spring gathering with the luscious salmon dish.

Butter sauce

2 shallots, finely chopped

1 bay leaf

4 peppercorns

2 cups dry white wine

2 tablespoons white wine vinegar

1 cup heavy cream

½ cup cold unsalted butter, cut into pieces

6 thin salmon fillets (approximately 5 ounces each)

olive oil

salt and pepper to taste

chopped fresh chives

To make sauce: In three-quart saucepan, over medium high heat, bring shallots, bay leaf, peppercorns, wine, and vinegar to a boil. Boil until the mixture is reduced to one-quarter of its original volume. Remove from heat. Add the cream and cold butter. Reheat over medium low heat, strain, and keep warm.

Brush the salmon with olive oil and season with salt and pepper. Grill the salmon. Depending on how hot your grill is, this will take 30 seconds to over a minute per side. The salmon should be pink in the center.

Ladle the sauce onto a warm plate. Sprinkle liberally with chopped chives. Arrange salon on top of the sauce. Serves 6.

Grilled Spring Lamb with Tomato-Herb

Cream Sauce

A fresh take on the old classic. For best results, stoke up a very hot charcoal fire, which will cook the meat quickly, keeping the center of the meat tender.

1 boned leg of spring lamb (about 3 pounds)

Marinade:

2 cups olive oil, or enough to cover the meat

1 clove garlic, minced

1 tablespoon dried mixed herbs, such as anise, basil, lavender, and rosemary

Sauce:

2 shallots, chopped

1 cup dry white wine

1 tablespoon white wine vinegar

1 bay leaf

6 peppercorns

1 cup heavy cream

1 cup cold unsalted butter, cut into small pieces

2 tomatoes

3 or 4 sprigs each basil, tarragon, chives, and thyme

Watercress for garnish

To make marinade: Mix olive oil, garlic, and mixed dried herbs in a medium-sized bowl. Slice leg of lamb into ½-inch-thick steaks. Put them in a large bowl and pour marinade over them. Cover and refrigerate for twenty-four hours.

Drain the steaks well; grill over very hot charcoal for about 2 to 3 minutes on each side to make the lamb medium-rare, 4 to 5 minutes to make it well done. Remember the meat continues to cook after you've removed it from the grill, so take the steaks off the fire just before they're cooked the way you want.

To make sauce: In 1-quart saucepan, over medium high heat, bring shallots, wine, vinegar, bay leaf, and peppercorns to a boil. Boil until mixture has reduced to one-third of the original volume. Add cream; whisk in butter until it melts. Strain the mixture into a small saucepan and keep warm.

Dip 2 tomatoes in boiling water for 5 seconds. Skin, seed, and dice. Coarsely tear basil, tarragon, chives, and thyme. Add the tomatoes and herbs to the sauce and let stand 5 minutes in a warm place, uncovered.

Spoon the sauce onto a warm plate and arrange the grilled lamb on top. Garnish with watercress. Serves 6.

Spring Treasure Hunt

Choose a date and location, get a group of families and friends together, then set them loose in your yard or home in search of eggs—both real, chocolate, and plastic filled with treats and trinkets.

Let guests know they've come to the right spot by hanging a welcome wreath on your garden gate or front door—perhaps a wire form covered in sheet moss and planted with live lobelia, primroses, and ivy. Wood violets are another fresh spring option. Then let the hunt begin. Let small children hunt for eggs first. Make sure they're not all so well hidden that they can't find them. Or make the hunt more exciting for older kids by making it a competition to see who can find the most. Yet another option is making teams of mixed age groups and assign-

ing each a color. The teams then have to hunt for eggs in their color. Taken together eggs can contain a set of clues to a hidden treasure. Award prizes to whatever team finds the treasure first.

At the post-treasure-hunt luncheon, decorate each place setting with miniature bouquets of lilies of the valley or violets, held in place around a napkin with a narrow silk ribbon or a piece of lace. Splash on the color: Paper lanterns and mesh butterflies could flutter overhead, whether dangling from a chandelier indoors or branches outside.

One of the fun activities could also be coloring eggs. There are a couple of ways to go:

*Substitute icing coloring (such as Wilton Icing Colors) for food coloring to achieve richer colors than you'd get with traditional Easter egg dyes. Brown eggs especially lend themselves to this look.

*Go natural: Onion skins tied around eggs give an orange marbled effect. Or create a dye bath from beets and cranberries for pink and red, spinach for delicate green.

*Achieve plaids and stripes by wrapping your oeufs in rubber bands, dental floss, and strips of narrow masking tape Alternatively, stamp with potato blocks and ink or poster paint.

*Layer colors by dipping eggs into progressively deeper shades. Rub with mineral oil for a soft sheen.

*Vary egg sizes. Go small with speckled quail eggs. Duck and goose eggs are double and triple the size of hen's eggs, respectively. Larger still, rhea, emu, and ostrich eggs are all sturdy enough to be carved and etched with a dremel tool and look great with metallic finishes. Emu eggs come already colored emerald green.

*Display them in a basket as your centerpiece, whether an old metal egg basket or an herb gathering type. Alternatively, nestle them in a graniteware bowl.

Thanksgiving

A Work Plan

Some would argue that the holidays that are completely devoted to food—and not gift giving—are the best of all. One of the best ways to savor Thanksgiving, of course, is as a potluck where everyone contributes a dish. Still, if you're the lucky host you'll need to do a little more advance planning than usual. The weekend before, you'll want to get out the serving dishes you'll need. Read through all the recipes to make sure you have all the ingredients you'll need. Make any soups you plan on serving. The day before, bake casseroles and prepare vegetable side dishes as well as desserts. On the morning of, prepare your turkey for the oven and set the dinner table after breakfast. In the afternoon, complete and warm up your side dishes, make gravy, and enjoy!

Freezing Tips:

*Equip your freezer with a thermometer so that you can do periodic temperature checks. It should read 0 degrees.

 *Since liquid expands as it freezes, leave extra room—about one inch—in soup and stew containers when going into the freezer.

*Thaw foods in the refrigerator for safety's sake. Defrosting at room temperature can lead to bacterial growth and spoilage.

*If you know you're going to cook food and put it directly in the freezer for later usage, undercook it slightly. That way, when you're reheating it you can cook it longer without overcooking it.

Turkey Talk

When buying turkey, figure on about 1 pound per person. The younger the turkey, the more tender the meat. Wild turkeys are another great option; your local butcher might be able to arrange one for you if you discuss it well in advance.

Before roasting turkey, remove the giblets (they are in the body or neck cavity) neck and liver. You can use the giblets and neck for stock, while the liver would be good cooked in a stuffing.

To prepare the bird, rinse and pat it dry, inside and out, using paper towels. Put it on a platter, covered, to catch juices. The United States Department of Agriculture (USDA) recommends buying a fresh turkey no more than 2 days before you're ready to use it and not defrosting frozen turkey until you're ready to use it. For frozen turkey defrosted in the refrigerator, allow one day of thawing for every four to five pounds of turkey. The USDA also suggests roasting at 325 degrees or higher, and checking the internal temperature with a meat thermometer. A cautious cook's rule of thumb: When the thickest part of the thigh reaches 180 degrees F on the thermometer, the turkey is done. Do not go by the color of the cooked meat, as it is not a surefire way to test doneness. After roasting, a turkey should stand for 15 to 20 minutes. This allows the juice to congeal and make carving a bit easier. Check the USDA website for up-to-date turkey tips www.fsis.usda.gov.

Autumn Decor

Thanksgiving tabletops don't have to be all turkeys and Pilgrims. Try a cabin in the woods theme. Line up a row of balsam-incense-burning log cabins you see at country gift shops. They look especially homey paired with a large-checked tablecloth.

Set up a Thanksgiving table with a variety of seasonal vegetables and wild things gathered from the woods. In addition to gourds, pumpkins, and squashes, try using mosses on a plate as a centerpiece, topped with acorns and honey locust pods. Set out woven baskets filled with pinecones and nuts.

Hollow out pumpkins as candleholders for a harvest celebration; for added color, cluster Savoy cabbages in rich mossy greens and electric purples. Fill a clear glass pantry jar with clementines.

For an intriguing centerpiece, consider bittersweet vines, which have naturally beautiful curves. Dynamic twists of this wild vine would make a surprising contrast with the serenity of a cultivated flower, such as peach-tinged white roses. Place in a container woven from palm fibers for even more textural contrast. Another option is to lay a

Menu

Appetizer

BALSAMIC GLAZED QUAIL STUFFED WITH SUN DRIED TOMATOES
AND WILD MUSHROOMS
FRENCH LENTIL AND CHORIZO RAGOUT

Salad

MERLOT POACHED FRENCH BUTTER PEAR WITH MAYTAG
BLUE CHEESE, BABY FRISEE AND HONEY GASTRIQUE

Entrée

GRILLED FILET MIGNON WITH CHILEAN SEA BASS,
BLACK TRUFFLE MASHED POTATOES, SUN DRIED TOMATO OLIVE
TAPENADE, GRILLED VEGETABLES

Viennese Dessert Tab...

BANANAS FOSTER PREPARED TO ORDER WTH VANIL...
CHOCOLATE SACHER TORTE, DULCE DE LECH...
CHESTNUT ST. HONO...
FRESH FRUIT TARTS & COCONUT C...
CHOCOLATE TRUFFLES & DOUBLE D...

COFFEE SERVICE, CAPPU...

grapevine wreath directly at the table's center. Combine herbs, tiny spears of red sumac, and chile peppers on the base. Don't cover it completely—the base is meant to show. By contrast, foam or straw wreaths work well with cranberries and rosehips because you can simply attach them by cutting toothpicks in half and using them to skewer berries to the wreath. Another option is to use floral glue. If you are using larger elements on such wreaths, such as apple, lay down a base of ivy leaves or some other foliage to camouflage the base completely. Decorate the sideboard with a huge dried gourd.

Round out the look with nature-inspired napkin rings. Assemble clusters of eucalyptus, autumn leaves, cinnamon sticks, and dried sage. Tie the aromatic bundles together and cinch around a napkin with raffia for a rustic look. For truly festive placecards, write guests' names in gold craft paint on bay leaves, tie a napkin with a lush velvet ribbon, and tuck each leaf inside. Another fun touch: Use a bay leaf coated with gold textile paint as a "stamp" for napkins.

Recipes

Cranberry Nachos

Here's an appetizer that gives Thanksgiving cranberries a completely new twist. The nacho chips laden with red and yellow pepper coulis, cranberry salsa, and goat cheese are arranged on a plate around a radicchio leaf "bowl" filled with still more cranberry salsa.

Red and Yellow Pepper Coulis (¼ cup each)

1 whole yellow bell pepper

1 whole red bell pepper

4 tablespoons olive oil

Salt and freshly ground pepper to taste

Cranberry Salsa:

½ cup cranberries

¼ cup fresh orange juice

¼ medium red onion, diced

1 fresh jalapeno pepper, diced

2 tablespoons chopped cilantro

¼ cup fresh lime juice

Pinch salt

Freshly ground pepper to taste

Sugar to taste

Nachos:

12 blue and gold tortilla chips

¼ pound mild goat cheese (chevre)

Radicchio

4 sprigs cilantro

Red and Yellow Pepper Coulis:

Char the whole peppers open over an open flame or under a preheated broiler. Place in a metal bowl and cover tightly with plastic wrap. Let sit for 15 minutes. Then wash off all charred skin and puree in 2 batches (one for each pepper) in the food processor until smooth. Drizzle olive oil over each coulis batch and season with salt and pepper.

Salsa:

Cook the cranberries in orange juice for 3 minutes, until tender. Place cranberry mixture in a bowl and add onion, jalapeno, and cilantro. Toss with lime juice and add salt, pepper, and sugar.

Nachos:

Preheat broiler. Arrange the blue and gold chips on a cookie sheet. To each chip, add 1 teaspoon each of the yellow and red pepper coulis and top with salsa and goat cheese, broken into pieces by hand. Put the pan under the broiler until the goat cheese softens (about 5 minutes, it can get slightly browned). Remove from the broiler. Arrange chips on serving plate. Form a bowl out of the radicchio leaves and fill with extra salsa. Garnish plate with cilantro sprigs and serve immediately. Serves 12.

Walnut-Wheatberry Salad

Here is a versatile salad that can be varied endlessly depending on what you have on hand. It's fun to put all the ingredients out and let guests mix their own salads. Plus, it's an easy make-ahead dish. This recipe serves a small crowd—as many as 15 guests.

1 pound wheatberries

1 cup chopped walnuts

Any or all of the following, to taste:

Thinly sliced red onion

Chopped scallions

Julienned orange zest

Golden raisins

Chopped parsley

Chopped mint

Pomegranate seeds

Salt and freshly ground pepper to taste

Recipes

Dressing:

½ cup each:

Walnut Oil

Vegetable Oil

Raspberry Vinegar

Cook the wheatberries by boiling in salted water until tender (this could take two hours or longer). Drain and cool to room temperature. Mix in the chopped nuts. Whisk the dressing ingredients together. Mix the salad ingredients together as desired, season to taste, and toss with the dressing.

Sweet Potato-Stuffed Maple Pork

The tartness of McIntosh apples combines with the sweetness of prunes and maple syrup to complement this festive pork roast, which could be served as a main course for a nontraditional holiday dinner.

 2 medium-size sweet potatoes

 2 pounds center-cut pork loin, butterflied

 1 clove garlic, slivered

 2 tablespoons melted butter

 ½ cup peel, chopped McIntosh apple

 2 teaspoons dried tarragon, or chopped fresh tarragon to taste

 12 pitted prunes

 6 strips bacon

 ⅓ to ½ cup pure maple syrup

 3 tablespoons apple cider or juice

 Preheat oven to 350 degrees F.

Bake the sweet potatoes for 35 minute, or until soft when pierced with a fork. Set aside to cool.

Trim any excess fat from the meat. Make random slits in the outside of the pork with the tip of a sharp knife and push a piece of garlic into each cut.

When the sweet potatoes are cool enough to handle, remove and discard their skins and mash them in 1 tablespoon of butter. Melt the other tablespoon of butter in a small frying pan over medium-low heat. Add the apple and tarragon and saute for 5 minutes, stirring constantly, until the apples are wilted. Mix into the mashed sweet potatoes.

Open the butterflied pork and place the prunes along the center line of the meat. Put the sweet potato mixture on

top of the prunes and pat into a cylinder. Fold the two sides of the meat up over the filling and tie the roast around the center and both ends. Place, cut side up, in a small roasting pan.

Wrap the bacon slices around the roast, tucking the ends underneath. Combine the maple syrup with the cider or juice and brush generously on the meat. Place the pork in the oven and roast for 1 hour, brushing on more of the maple glaze every 10 to 15 minutes. The meat is done when it reaches 170 degrees F. (Be sure your meat thermometer is stuck into the meat, not the filling.)

Remove the roast from the oven and let it sit at room temperature for a few minutes before slicing. Serves 6-8.

Apple Gingerbread

Here is a new twist on gingerbread. The apple adds a delightful contrast. Using clean, flat fall leaves as "stencils," decorate the top with confectioner's sugar for a beautiful harvest presentation.

1 ½ cups flour

1 teaspoon baking soda

½ teaspoon salt

1 teaspoon ground ginger

½ teaspoon ground allspice

¼ teaspoon ground cloves

Pinch nutmeg

Pinch cardamom

½ cup butter, softened

¼ cup firmly packed light brown sugar

¼ cup firmly packed dark brown sugar

2 eggs

2 tablespoons plus 1 teaspoon molasses

½ cup milk

1 large apple, peeled, cored, and coarsely chopped

Confectioner's sugar for garnish

Whipped cream for garnish

Preheat oven to 350 degrees F. Butter and flour an 8-inch round cake pan and set aside.

Recipes

Sift together the flour, baking soda, salt, and spices and set aside. In a large bowl, cream the butter and light and dark brown sugars with an electric mixer. Beat in the eggs, one at a time, add the molasses, and beat well. Add the flour mixture in thirds, alternating with the milk, beating after each addition. (The batter will be lumpy.)

Pour the batter into the prepared pan. Scatter the chopped apple on the batter and push the piece down until they are almost covered.

Bake for 35 minutes and test with a cake tester or toothpick. If the tester does not come out clean, bake for another 5 minutes. Remove the gingerbread from the oven, loosen the sides with a knife, and cool completely on a wire rack. To decorate, place a doily or some flat leaves on top of the cake and sift confectioners sugar over them to create a pattern. Remove the doily or leaves and serve the gingerbread with whipped cream, if desired. Serves 8.

Chapter 8. Celebrations

Weddings: Styling at Home

Nothing compares with the at-home wedding for extravagance. The challenge is to take an ordinary home and turn it into a stage for romance. Not only must the dining table or buffet be dressed to the hilt, but every corner of the home must be nothing less than magical.

If the wedding is in winter, use the fireplace or a large floral screen as a backdrop for the ceremony. This is especially beautiful if you marry by candlelight, with votives placed on windowsills, candelabra on the mantel, and wall sconces flickering with tapers. Or create the illusion of a garden indoors using potted ficus trees, patio shrubs, hanging fuchsia, and ordinary houseplants. Bring a trellis or latticework indoors and wind it through with ivy or silk flower garlands. Add wicker furniture and you've created an inviting, weatherproof sanctuary.

So that you'll be able to prepare the home for the big event in advance, use dried flowers as much as possible (no wilting!). For instance, decorate a hallway with wall pockets filled with dried poppy pods and lavender. For a home wedding or anniversary event, ornament a banister with a delicate garland of air-dried sweet Annie, wild grasses, sage, and small bouquets of yarrow and tansy. To construct the garland, bunch tiny bouquets together with florist's wire. Then take a long wire and begin wrapping it around the base of each bundle; conceal the join by overlapping. An everlasting's wreath hanging above the mantel would be dreamy in a pale palette with touches of silver and celadon.

It's amazing what fabric can do to dress up a room. Dinner tables could be swathed in shimmering aqua floral brocade, ordinary fold-up chairs disguised with cotton slipcovers. For a cozy sense of enclosure outdoors, encircle a tent with summery fabrics. Tables there might wear cotton duck, quilted linen, and ticking runners. In autumn, toss a plaid lap blanket or a patterned shawl over a solid-covered fabric. Interesting wallpaper remnants could serve as runners.

Flower Magic

*Mass together one inexpensive flower—like carnations, dahlias, or daisies—for centerpieces

*Feature a single flower in tabletop arrangements, like white calla lilies in a low white pot or white anthurium in a square clear glass vase combined with a nonfloral material like marabou boa or plumes. Another way to add interest is to color the water or to use aquarium gravel/sand in alternating layers of color.

*Create a centerpiece that is a planted garden of grasses (much like the wheatgrass you see at the green market) with individual flowers like California poppies in florist's vials "planted" throughout

*Hand-decorate containers. Plain yellow vases could be transformed with a smattering of graphic red polka dot stickers

*For a "clubby" centerpiece, strew petals around a mercury glass lamp base with beaded shade

*Top moss with votives in a zinc or wooden box. It makes an artful centerpiece

*Use vines like jasmine, ivy, asparagus fern, and stephanotis curving around a metal or wood framework as a wedding backdrop, perhaps for the ceremony. Tuck in clusters of oranges

*Cover silver candelabra with twisted vines. These could dress up a buffet table

*Create all-green centerpieces, with kale heads, hydrangea, and herbs in urns that are covered with moss (greens are generally a fraction of the price of flowers)

*Fill footed silver containers or mint julep cups with camellia leaves and clusters of gardenias surrounded by 4 tall tapers (surrounding any center-piece with tapers amplifies the effect)

*Fill pedestal bowls with lemons, limes, granny smith apples, or pears, accent-ed with lemon leaves; contrast the tablecloth with the fruit, for instance Tiffany blue with lemons

*For an outrageous (and dirt cheap) design, plant a tabletop garden of wheatgrass grown from wheatberries. In ten days it's ready. Then on your plot of soil, tube flowers in florist's vials (try inexpensive, long-lasting ger-bera daisies).

*If you can't afford an expensive arrangement, keep it simple on pur-pose. Maybe you'll just float a few flowers in a pretty bowl, surrounded by votives.

White on White

The color white is a universe unto itself. Pure, pearly shades are cottagey and light, freshening up whatever they surround. Ivory and parchment hues impart an antique aura. White is never boring. Regal trimmed with gold, it becomes whimsical paired with pink. With this all-purpose color as the foundation of your tabletop and dining area, you'll always have the perfect setting.

When you layer white on white, the eye gravitates toward subtle details. Textures become more pronounced. Whether the scalloped border on a porcelain teaset or the handiwork of a lace cloth, small touches stand out.

A collection of white shades creates an oasis of warmth and festivity. Paint ordinary wooden folding chairs white for an elegant look. Mix several shades of white in china and linens, paired with crystal bowls and goblets to catch the light.

Mingle creamware with salt-glazed stoneware or porcelain on an all-pale china tabletop. Or use it with pastels—lavender, peach, seafoam—for a spring-time look. Add a touch of gold for sparkle. Mix your grandmother's heir-loom gold-rimmed Wedgwood with plain white soup bowls. In your antiquing travels, pick up plates with gold initials and have fun matching them to your guests' names.

For an all-white look on a budget, paint exteriors of water bottles with several coats of white high gloss paint and use them as vases.

Creative Way to Use Collections

Looking for ways to creatively reuse objects from the past? Consider the following:

*Pierced cake baskets could hold a cornucopia of vegetables themed to the season, such as baby peas and carrots in spring, tiny squash and pumpkins in fall

*Biscuit barrel and muffin baskets can easily be turned into ice buckets at your next party

*Antique tosat racks make elegant napkin holders or display pieces for menu cards

*Old-fashioned ice cream "boats"—the kind used to serve banana splits—are fabulous for serving olives or hors d'oeuvres

*Create a tablescape using varied sizes and interesting shapes of vases and cylinders. Unite the look by swathing them in the same fabric

Chandelier Enchantment

Scout flea markets for secondhand chandeliers that could be brought outdoors, setting an instantly romantic mood. Of course, chandeliers both indoors and out could be decorated outrageously:

*Hang colorful paper lanterns

*Weave in feather boas

*Dangle colored crystals, charms, ribbons, shells

*Drape faux pearl and crystal necklaces

*Hang a mixed bag of utilitarian trinkets including spectacles and keys

*Entwine vine tendrils like honeysuckle, ivy, bittersweet, and wild grape.

Outdoor Aisle Markers

Define an aisle or party area on your lawn with any of the following:

*Shells

*Torches

*Large topiaries

*River rocks

*Maypoles with tulle and ribbons

*Small evergreens wired with lights

*Candelabra

*Assorted Oriental carpets

*Hurricane lanterns

*Pinwheels

*Luminaria with electric tea lights

*Stone garden cherubs

*Buckets or baskets of fruit or herbs

*Haybales

*Bells

*Paper lanterns on shepherd's crooks

*Buddhist prayer flags

Ten Flowers That Won't Wilt in the Sun

1. peegee hydrangea

2. aster

3. mums

4. marigold

5. zinnia

6. mini-calla and Oriental lilies

7. dendrobium and cymbidium orchids

8. lisianthus

9. sunflower

10. dahlia

Birthdays, Anniversaries And Other Milestones

Celebrate life's milestones with a fabulous theme. Indulge in the offbeat and the unexpected. Strike a nostalgic note for an anniversary. Decorate with memorabilia to set a nostalgic theme at an anniversary. A sixties theme with a fringed tablecloth and tie-dyed napkins works beautifully for a couple married in the hippie era. Or decorate napkins with little bracelets of wire strung with number beads spelling out the year they got married.

For a birdwatcher's birthday, display vintage binoculars or a whimsically painted birdhouse on a stack of birding books as a centerpiece. Pay tribute to a gardener with an outdoor-inspired tabletop. Terracotta plant plates could be chargers. Invert water glasses and tuck single daisy heads underneath at each place setting or weave a daisy chain along chairbacks. Arrange contoured layers of crepe paper over a white tablecloth to look like flowers petals. Graduations also spark creativity. You could make a centerpiece of pennants or cinch the napkin at each tablesetting with a tassel.

Dessert Celebration

To host a large, splashy celebration but keep the budget in check, consider a dessert-only party or reception. It could be as simple as serving only mint chocolate chip ice cream and champagne. There are several bonuses to this approach. You won't have to worry about ordering a huge cake that needs to be transported to your home. It saves money and eliminates untold hours in the kitchen. You can still have your cake, of course. Why not create a "dessert gazebo" indoors or out. Fill pastry stands with a multitude of small cakes: German chocolate, Italian cream cake, lemon poppyseed, carrot cake—even Danish wedding cookies. Or pass a trio of minidesserts on a large-size dinner plate. Cream puffs, a sorbet with berries, and a chocolate pâté are an appealing combination. Use fruit as a vessel in which to serve something luscious. Imagine a custard-filled navel orange garnished with sprigs of mint. Or scooped-out pineapple shells topped with lightly baked meringue rosettes. For decoration, place herbal topiaries of sage and rosemary on the buffet and scatter gardenia or rose blossoms on the table at the last minute for amazing fragrance. If you truly must have a big cake, rather than hiring a cake designer to create pricey sugar roses, use real, pesticide-free flowers instead (they're actually cheaper). Tie a real ribbon around the cake as a decoration.

Giving Thanks And Making Toasts

Celebrations often call for someone to make a toast. It could be as simple as saying, "Thanks to everyone for coming." Or it could be a heartfelt speech. Traditionally, toasting takes place after everyone has gone through the buffet line or has been served dinner. Another option is to toast during cocktails or after everyone has been served champagne. At weddings, there is a protocol to follow. The best man toasts first, followed by the groom, then the bride, parents, and whoever else wants to speak. It is also considered correct for the hosts of the reception—the parents of the bride or groom—to speak first, perhaps offering a short welcome toast. A few toasting pointers:

*Only the toaster stands up to speak. The toastee always remains seated. Other guests can also sit.

*Recall a funny or poignant memory of the person you're toasting.

But don't go on for more than three or four minutes.

*To toast a person simply and eloquently, go with "To Your Health" or its many foreign translations, such as the French "A votre santé" or the Spanish "Salud."

* "I would like you to join me in drinking a toast to two wonderful people" works as well for weddings as anniversaries, engagement parties, and rehearsal dinners.

Credits

Speciality Foods

Meat & Game

D'Artagnan
www.dartagnan.com
(800) 327-8246
marinated duck breast

The HoneyBaked Ham Company
www.honeybaked.com
(866) 492-HAMS
Spiral-sliced ham and glazed turkey
breast--perfect for your buffet

Lobel's
www.lobels.com
(877) 783-4512
natural prime beef

Sam's Butcher Shop
www.samsbutchershop.com
(570) 842-9707
specialty meats

Fish & Seafood

Bold Coast Smokehouse
www.boldcoastsmokehouse.com
(888) 733-0807
Scandinavian gravlax, cold smoked lox

Browne Trading Company
www.brownetrading.com
http://www.brownetrading.com/
(800) 944-7848

Perona Fams
www.peronafarms.com
(800) 750-6190
smoked Atlantic salmon

Oils, Vinegars & Preserves

Anamarie Organic Olive Oil
www.anamarieorganicoliveoil.com
(845) 635-2530
Portuguese olive oil, olives, vinegars

Chef Shop
www.chefshop.com
(800) 596-0885
artisan vinegars, bing cherries

Gustiamo
www.gustiamo.com
(877) 907-2525
citrus marmalades

Stonewall Kitchen
www.stonewallkitchen.com
(800) 207-JAMS
raspberry peach champagne jam, wild
Maine blueberry jam
roasted garlic and onion jam

Cheese

Cow Girl Creamery
www.cowgirlcreamery.com
(866) 433-7834
organic artisan cheeses

Mozzarella Company
www.mozzco.com
cow's and goat's milk cheeses, samplers
(800) 798-2954

Sprout Creek Farm
www.sproutcreekfarm.org
(845) 485-9885
farm-made European-style cheeses

Savory Treats

Bella Cucina Artful Food
www.bellacucina.com
(800) 580-5674
pestos for pasta, antipasti, and sauces;
Italian olives; dipping crackers and
mustards

Farm Country Soups
www.farmcountrysoup.com
(866) 877-SOUP
elegant, dinner-party-quality soups

Frog Hollow Farm
www.froghollow.com
(888) 779-4511
turnovers in many flavors, including
leek and mushroom, ham and gruyere;
also fresh fruit

Hancock Gourmet Lobster Company
www.hancockgourmetlobster.com
(800) 552-0142
elegant lobster rolls

Ruthie & Gussie's
www.ruthieandgussies.com
(877) 4-LATKES
traditional potato pancake batter for
Hanukkah and beyond...

Dessert

Dancing Deer Baking Co.
www.dancingdeer.com
(888) 699-DEER
brownies, gingerbread cake, mixes

David Bouley
www.davidbouley.com
(212) 964-2525
lemon tea cake

Empire Torte Company
www.empiretorte.com
(800) 908-6783
intense chocolate tortes

My Boulangerie
myboulangerie.com
(360) 421-1618
authentic French pastries and croissants

Polly's Cakes
www.pollyscakes.com
(888) 386-1221
outrageously beautiful fondant cakes